On The Cruz

Other works by Ron Lampi

Bay of Monterey, Poems of Monterey Bay 2010
Toward The Mythos, philosophical essays 2010

Other works from River Sanctuary Publishing:

From the Corridors (of the Labyrinth) 2011

The Poet Reflects 2012

Through the Labyrinth: A Guided Astrological Meditation 2013

Poetry / Is 2013

A Divine Psyche Manifesto & other poems 2016

The Edge Manifesto 2018

Photons 2018

Technos & Psyche, A Prelude & other poems 2019

Lamp Light, A selection of short poems 3rd ed. 2020

The Vision of Psyche & other poems 3rd ed. 2020

The New Age Vision 2021

The New Story: Preludes 2nd ed. 2021

The Golden Thread 2022

On The Cruz

Poems of Santa Cruz

1988-2021

2nd edition 2022

including

Inside the Vortex (of Santa Cruz)

The Cruz & other poems

The Great Santa Cruz Mountains Earthquake

Ron Lampi

On The Cruz
Copyright © 2022 by Ron Lampi
New edition; first published 2012

All rights reserved. No part of this book may be reproduced, stored in a retrieval system, or transmitted, in any form or by any means, electronic, mechanical, photocopying, recording, or otherwise, without the written prior permission of the author, except in the case of brief quotations embodied in critical articles and reviews.

Cover design by River Sanctuary graphic arts
Cover photographs by Ron Lampi

ISBN 978-1-952194-21-4
Printed in the United States of America

Additional copies are available from:
www.riversanctuarypublishing.com
amazon.com

RIVER SANCTUARY PUBLISHING
P.O Box 1561
Felton, CA 95018
www.riversanctuarypublishing.com
Dedicated to the awakening of the New Earth

Contents

I

Sing, She said...3
Just say you're from…..4
Who sees the city...5
Is Santa Cruz……...6
Change, change…..7
What I have set out…..8
Who is There to Remember?..9
The Community A Vision..11
It Happens Here..14
Ocean Street: Welcome to The Cruz.............................16
Town Clock...19
Beginning from Pacific Avenue....................................21
Night Cruz'n Pacific Avenue..30
The Avenue is Empty...36
Pacific Avenue Alive Again..37
Santa Cruz the Bubble..39
Santa Cruz *The Cruz*..41
This Cruz...45
A Lotta Talk..47
An Old Illusion...48
Find Yourself a Vision..50
The Poet-Who-Walks...52
Café Cruz'n...54
Survival Mode...58
Tents..61
Parade into First Night...62
A New Years Day Tradition..65
Pacific Ave Halloween..69
That She inspires..71
Pride Day..72

Wharf to Wharf 74
Beach Boardwalk July 4th 76
A Summertime Summer Night 83
Romantic at Capitola Beach 86
An Afternoon in Felton 88
Full Moon in June 89
The Seers Circle 93
Upon leaving the bookstore 95
Synergy Party 96
Driving Highway 17 98
The Acacias 102
Bonny Doon 103

II

Inside the Vortex (of Santa Cruz) 2005

The Vortex 109
Inside the Vortex 110

III

The Cruz & other poems 1988-1990 / 2016

The Cruz 125
Caffé Pergolesi 141
Café Caméléon 148
The Happy Hour Gang 154
Doctor's Advice 163
Now I'm In It 165

IV

The Great Santa Cruz Mountains Earthquake – a poem chronicle 1989-1990

Quake At 5:04 175
A Small Victory 186
To Build Again 196

V
A Season of Fire 2020-2021

The CZU Lightning Complex Fire 203
The Freak Storm 204
Falling Ash 206
Our Martian Sky 208
We Now Know… 209
A Snapshot as I Sit 210

VI

Happy Hour: The Catalyst 215
Pontiac Grill: Memory Corridor...................218
Opening Day Saturn Cafe............................222
Al Dente: The Experience............................225
The Ugly Mug: The Ultimate Café 228
Ciao Bella: Restaurant Eccentric.................232
India Joze: Joe's Own Style 237
Kianti's Fridays 240
Norma Jean's Coffee: The Name................. 242
The White Raven: 245
Your Mountain Town Hangout Café 245
A Mr. Toots Evening................................... 248
Sip Sip: Mutari Chocolate............................250
Little Café Delmarette 253
Go Ask Alice 254
Pergolesi is Closing 256
Storefront Logos Still 259
Taqueria Vallarta... 260
Rio is Dead…but— 261
Now *The Union*..263
Felix Kulpa Gallery 266
41st Avenue Shop Shop Shop 268
Pizza My Heart 275

The Farmers' Scene 276
Food Not Bombs 281
Remember that Comedy Scene? 284
The E3: A Short Story 286
Hula Hula 290
Luminescence: a Spa & *Kava Bar* *292*
The Rave 294

VII

I am doing what a poet… *299*
They're Dude'n It 300
The Gique of Bubbles 303
Magic Man/Magic Geeks 305
 He's on a Mission Caravan 309
The Street Poet 312
Brandon: The Ringleader 314
George 318
Eucalyptus Man 320
Café Fast One 324
Kelsey 325
To Rose 326
Shelton 327
Deep South Voice 328
The Great Morgani 329
Slow way down *331*
An Epiphany of Pink 332
Balloon Wizard Mark 335
Lost Poets Salon 337
And Alan "Sitar" Brown *339*
Mr. TV 341
Calls Himself Nicho 342
A Hit'a Words 344

Art Opening(s) 345
Sheila's Outrage – Outreach 348
The Day Gilda Died... 352
Jack O'Neill Memorial Paddle Out 354
I Look at a Map.. 357
The Soul of The Cruz 359

About The Author 361

A companion collection to *On The Cruz* is *Bay of Monterey, Poems of Monterey Bay*. Both collections present the parallel running inspirations that begin to bring into form the Mythos of place, which today is fundamental to the emerging Mythos of the New Age. And there is another work *The Giant Santa Cruz Poem* that one must imagine weaving itself through both collections. Also, my experience of street performance on Pacific Avenue is documented in another collection of poems *The Multi Guy on Pacific Ave*. Last, references to the Vision are to my Vision of Psyche. Among other works in which it is presented, see in particular the work *The Vision of Psyche*.

I

Sing, She said,
Sing of this place
that out of your heart
  has grown...

Just say you're from Santa Cruz
when you're out traveling the country somewhere,
    & then smile—

Oh, yes! Santa Cruz! I wish I were there too…

Who sees the city
        in all its diversity?
Who
        in the heart
                is deep enough
                        to open to?
Who celebrates it?

A varied Song that all might enjoy—

Is Santa Cruz—*today*—
The Cruz we have always known?
You will hear them say
it is not the same
as years ago,
        so much of this place
     comes & goes—
And is something lost?
Has something been lost?

Change, change, always that swept along feeling of change…

The culture changes, the collective changes,
the times change & Postmodern must change,
rapidly now the future, as they say, comes upon us,

       yet, The Cruz—
something here

    about this place

because Mythos has touched it,

    lives

       in the soul

& out of soul

    is a special place

        still

January 2008

Change, change…

Change, change, always that swept along feeling of change
—especially here, this place The Cruz, a vortex,
   in a swirrrrl—

                             Day & night
    the surf is such sweet sound in our ears,
you get so used to it,
          don't realize,
    this subtle & perpetual power,
      so near
             —the universal solvent as Neptune is—,
that we are immersed in it,
              swimming in it,
   like the Moon,
  some fixity of ours/stability/conditioning/assumption/belief
       is always dissolving,
   we are always dissolving,
        always changing, changing,
  no end to, no end—
        Better find your Self / your center

What I have set out to do,
in this art I have come to practice,
    its intent,
is to weave the Threads of place,
beginning this place The Cruz,
that others might come to see
how it was & why
        The Mythos
   was born here,
in the livingness of this place,
out of the fruitfulness of its time,
   The Mythos,
       spoken through me
    & weaving through me,
its Golden Thread,
      the dispensation *of* Time,
that the Whole of all we are,
     this ever-weaving of Web,
  this Melody
that's all around us
      & moving through us
  —this Melody I hear—
that the Poet I am
would utter the Song of it—

    the Word—

  its Mythos of place

I am here

   to sing

September 2003

Who is There to Remember?

Who is there to remember all there is to remember
    a place was,
            & is, now,
      how places are always changing, changing—

Who is there to remember?
Is it the local historian?
              Does the local historian,
remembering the past, bring into play
    all the Threads of place?
What *are* the Threads of place that weave
    what it was,
           & is, now,
      how it's changing, changing,
         Threads that are always weaving—
Does the historian speak from the firsthand *Mythos*
    of place?

Is it the old-timer who remembers?
The old-timer shares a long memory, to be sure,
but is it formed by the universality
                  of an archetypal
           Memory?
By an art of Melody & Vision that would bring it
    into originary presentation?
The old-timer has seen a lot, we can be certain—
But many are the Threads to be woven
    of a Mythos
          that Time weaves.
    Oh, perhaps
a videographer has captured something of a place,
    a visual slice of the Mythos of place,
over time a select record of people, locations, events.
But is there a Story of all the Threads
              that weave a place?

Who is there to present Memory, Mythos of all there is
   of all the Threads
         to remember,
                  before the community?
Who is there to help the community in a collective
   remembering?
Who has seen the Threads with an Eye behind the eyes?
Who has through Psyche experienced the Threads
   woven into place?
Who has the Ear & Eye to weave the language
   of Threads,
         to remember
                  all there is to remember?

Must it not be the poet?
Does the poet not, still, have a role
   in the community?

July 2006

The Community A Vision

The community a Vision the poet is called to build
    from the heart of us going outward,
        a Thread woven throughout the Fabric
  of what is,
        transforming it
    from the inside
as snakelike moving along irrepressibly
          to become
    what must be,
if the sense of our belonging together
        —today—
    is to cohere,
if true justice of place be done,
    even when,
        telling it like it is,
someone must take account,
        be the Mythos-maker

        the Word

        we live by—

The Word has come,
it lives through my Song,
    a Thread of Gold
        in the stream—
Look—
& you will see it flashing
        as the waters
          around it
      against rock
    splash & flow—

The Word has come,
here, on *The Cruz*—
 The Cruz—
  the sign
   of an Age
  dismembered & dying...
   & it's such a slow death—
  but someday,
   new named,
    new born,
   someday will be—

   And so I, too,
  was dismembered
    & died
   on *The Cruz*,
   & was reborn
    through Vision,
  a new Seed of me
   out of Monterey Bay,
    out of her submarine canyon depths,
  I planted in the heart,
   in the heart
    of *The Cruz*

 where it begins,
 this place
  birthplace of Vision
  where Psyche the Word was born,
  where Technos—today's God—
  looms
   from over the mountain
    to encounter Psyche,
   our new Divinity to be
   —we will witness the confrontation—,
 this place
  where the Integration of us must happen
   here,
    in our New Age Athens.

This place The Cruz I see before me,
circumscribed of Santa Cruz Mountains, Monterey Bay
    & Pacific Ocean—
Here, the creative mash stirs of surfers & fishermen, farmers & poets,
of dancers, writers, artists & musicians, street people & performers,
of entrepreneurs & restaurateurs, of high-tech geeks, students
    & student perennials,
of inventors & fringe scientists, of small & local business owners,
of hemp activists, ecoactivists, feminists, astrologers, psychics,
of Wiccans, pagans, Buddhists, evangelists, Rastafarians,
    of college instructors & UC professors,
of alternative health practitioners, herbalists & healers,
of meditators, spiritual teachers, retirees & time-warp children
    of the Sixties,
& all folk of conventional ways who make up community—

I have partaken of it.

1999

It Happens Here

Do not tell me it cannot happen here—
It happens wherever Spirit chooses to strike.

Do not tell me New York, San Francisco,
LA or Chicago, Sedona or Boulder,
or the Postmodern capital of the planet—
deconstructed Europe, the castrated of Spirit.

Birth of new life requires proper soil, the right time,
auspicious conditions, a destined need, a crisis, a death,
and—if only one—an individual prepared
    to be struck,
        taking it
            in
  a Walk-in
        of Spirit.

Spirit strikes & strikes again—
All it takes is one
      standing there
           in the OPEN
—& hopefully, will not others join
          & stand there

        in the OPEN?

I say,
It happens here—
    in Santa Cruz
        north end Monterey Bay
           state of California
              in the US of A
    at the cliff edge of Western civilization.

I say,
It happens here
    as Mother Gaia steps now
            onto the stage
                of the galaxy—

I am taking you on *The Cruz*.

The Intelligences approve.

1999

Ocean Street: Welcome to The Cruz

Comin' down the lush, twisty, mountain-treacherous corridor
    of Highway 17,
        just before exit Pasatiempo,
            a glimpse of our Goddess—
the smooth-skinned Bay shimmering in the distance,
rimmed by pale blue silhouetted mountains southward Monterey;
& there's another glimpse after a curve or two,
        & then Goddess is there again a straight view,
as simultaneously the first unmistakable of Cruz landmarks,
    to the right,
        is prominent above all—
      the midtown steeple of Holy Cross Church,
& then suddenly an underpass, the highway ends
    —there's a traffic light—& cars pour onto Ocean Street
      & it's
        Welcome to Santa Cruz
                the sign says.
And for all who drive down
this main drag into town, for the record, these, the following,
    are the sights
        of Year 2000:
Hard right at the light—Bailey Properties, a Denny's,
the new, coming soon, Hampton Inn, & then various motels
—Best Western, National 9, & some other—on the left;
then back & forth, to the right & left, couple gas stations,
    a donut shop, Steve's Music World,
Midas Auto Service, a low profile McDonald's, a floral shop,
Too Much Fun party headquarters, Baker's Square,
    Beach City Gas,
Marianne's Ice Cream, Quality Inn, another National 9,
    Kelly Moore Paints,
then some houses on the left, a Budget car rental,
there's some nondescript automotive place, Togo's an eatery,
    Santa Cruz Diner on the right,
then a major intersection, Water Street comes up—

                        At the four corners are
gas stations Chevron & Shell, showy window Bridal Concepts,
    & a Washington Mutual;
                        then comes
the big blockhouse Santa Cruz County Governmental Center
    set back from a big parking lot;
across the street, the Morgan Stanley Dean Witter building,
The Jury Room bar, New Wing Wah Chinese Restaurant,
    there's a Jack in the Box, Avis, Staircase Tatoo,
Doctors on Duty on the right again, next a tall, generic Holiday Inn,
a First Church of Christ Scientist & California State Parks
    office building, left,
                        then, crossin' the aqueduct—
Mei Garden Chinese Cuisine, a row of business buildings,
    The Islander Motel, Travelodge,
                & next with a rise in the street
you're passin' Best Western, Thai House, you're at the corner
    of Soquel—
It's Rock'N Tacos, part of a little shopping complex,
other corner a 76 station, there's another Chevron, Continental Inn,
    & then a slight curve in Ocean
        & suddenly—a short distance ahead—the famous
                Giant Dipper roller coaster appears, like some
                    otherworld apparition,
& still you're passing King Chwan Chinese Restaurant,
a little Farmers Insurance building, Ocean Animal Clinic next,
    there's a big old house on the right,
& suddenly now there's a dip in Ocean crossing Broadway
    & there's an Inn Cal, a 7 Eleven,
suddenly it's houses, low rent cottages, Las Esperanza Market,
    & seemingly out-of-place here,
                the pillared Guesthouse Pacific Inn
    set-off like its own, potted plant, fortress,
& then more cottages, little corner Ocean Market on the left
    at the stop sign at Barson,
        a just opening taqueria off to the right,
            a "for sale," long-time boarded-up bar across from it,
& the opposite corner, a low-lying, shrub-hidden office building,
    then it's residential all the way

17

     to East Cliff Drive/San Lorenzo Boulevard
  —& don't let that fool you, a proper boulevard it isn't.
This is where Ocean Street ends, here, at the light,
       the San Lorenzo River is here,
   channeled by engineered banks
     the other side of which
  across a broad, summertime bustling, parking lot
   is the sought-after amusement land
     of the Santa Cruz Beach Boardwalk.

    And when tourist season hits
or it's simply a gorgeous weather weekend,
it's all bumper to bumper the whole length
of this welcome-to-The-Cruz main drag into town.
It could be Ocean Street into just about Anytown USA,
  as you can see—
You would never guess, would you, comin' in this way,
how different of a world this Cruz really is,
but just wait,
    you'll see—

September 2000

Town Clock

Axis of the city
        (& more—
It is anchored here,
      north end of downtown
          N. Pacific Ave,
its 4 clock faces
       facing out
          4 directions
    above the chimney-bricked 4 arches,
   a white tower rising higher,
        U.S. flag highest of all,
     outlined at night
            in white lights.
   And *below*—
         an up-rushing of waters—
Little does the public know
    the round basin fountain
       under the vaulted arches,
modestly into the air gushing
      like a geyser pulsing,
is foundation symbol of the New Age—
              It is here,
  at the heart of The Cruz,
   at the axis,
      at the point of beginnings—
Do multitudes not flock here New Years
            at midnight?
Thousands throng First Night
      to this point of beginnings,
our solar time keeper, Saturn cross-bound
              Town Clock,
      this point/place
   of memorial gathering
  when the Year to come
          is born.

At the heart of The Cruz—
    A tower built to time.
But more fundamental
       than suffering the Cross
           is primordial Time,
  how it gushes forth—
            continuous creation

    The Fountain

September 2000

Beginning from Pacific Avenue

Our snaky-winding & flower child of an era, pre-Quake
Pacific Garden Mall   of   years   gone   by!
is now a post-Quake straight-out-moneyed decorator tree-lit-lined
               tourist boulevard—
New buildings still go up seasonally where others came down;
new businesses come & go—now you see them & now they go—;
always there're new faces, always new exchanges & rendezvous,
  always new intentions & big plans,
always new pipe dreams & crashes & existential resurrections,
& a flood of memories come back as I cruise along this path,

       Pacific Avenue—

  Heart of our city!

And faithfully I will walk our Avenue & all the streets of the heart
  for you,
I will sing on this Cruz, as best I can sing, a Thread of Song
  winding throughout its life,
I will observe all, noting characters along the way, naming names,
remembering as I can of what once was, anecdotes relating
  of so-and-so & so-and-so,
         spinning vignettes of reverie;
& even our local businesses I will name & bring alive for you.

Here is our canvas, this place, *this magical place*,
  as Norma once said,
where the paints are plenty—

      Yes, I remember,
I was driving on my way out of town,
I stopped at the traffic light at Water & Pacific,
four people stood beneath the Town Clock,
  (& through the years various protesters with signs & banners
    have stood beneath our landmark Town Clock)
four people stood there on that day, a family perhaps,
  out having some local commentary fun—

It was Mom, Dad, a boy & a girl, lined up in a row,
all dressed in these prim scout trooper uniforms,
& each held up a blank white sign for all to see—
Imagine that

      BLANK WHITE SIGNS

One motorist yelled out, not comprehending,
    "What's it say?"
"Whatever!" replied the girl.

                  —So it goes.
—*Only in Santa Cruz,* as they say—

           Whatever

                      And so it goes—
Every day the building of the heart goes outward—
You sit a few moments on the Avenue as I do now
& all the regulars of this world begin to saunter by...

                      Say, for example,
a man—for some reason—happens to spot me, he stops,
he's slight bent by age, sporting a San Francisco Giants ball cap
    & tweed sports jacket,
& he asks me about Clinton, actually a gambit to share
    his opinion, but that's alright;
he says,
    It's none of the government's damn business what Clinton did,
& he couldn't remember me now, could he?
            15 years ago Community Hospital
he would stop in after joggin' & chatter awhile.

          And only moments later, there's another—
the once computer geek who abandoned tons of boxes
of belongings at our house over 3 years ago, before I moved in,
I see him walk by, often I see him play chess with others, here,
at the Santa Cruz Coffee Roasting Company, where I now sit,

—he has no idea what became of his stuff—
                              but I see him
always wandering the Avenue, & once again I'll probably
see him play chess, here, at the Coffee Roasting Company...

          And sooner or later,
if you're downtown enough,
you're bound to encounter really bent-over Wilma
—well, that's what I first called her, not really knowing her name,
but found out later her name is Jean—,
                    it's usually the back of her head,
a mass of thick blonde hair hangin' over, hidin' her face,
she's in her heavy black coat, has inward bent legs,
her trusty bike weighed down with bags never far,
she rides around town all day oblivious to others,
perhaps more dangerous, she's oblivious to cars,
with all that hair, bent over so, it's a wonder
     she can see.

                    And how many remember ol' Tom Scribner,
he's immortalized in sculpture now in front of Bookshop Santa Cruz,
playin' a saw as you would see him in the late 70s play,
there, in the little hippy corner park across from the Town Clock,
     next the old Common Ground coffee hang-out
          twanging there his geee-tar saw—
                    How many remember him?

          And Kosmic Lady
once proselytized on the ol' Mall,
a one-time social worker, then, at some point, something
     had changed for her—
You would see her shouldering a huge astro-prophetic mandala cross
preaching the Good News of these new times
                    that UFO people were here—
She had a wedding ceremony once, tying a loose knot with a guy
     name of Morning Star
                    —short-lived it turned out—;
the ceremony though I remember took place
                in the short-lived Phoenix New Age Café

      where the Coffee Roasting Company went in,
                           that was, before the Quake—
I remember 'cause Sylvia & I had announced it New Years '78
on the radio waves of KZSC—
            (must'a been Elizabeth Gips' program then)
Like, everyone out there listening was welcome to the ceremony.

          And now I find Mr. Twister,
who gained recent national media fame
with his, as the slogan went,
          Mr. Twister, Feed my meter—
A parking meter ordinance infraction
   got him
       some big attention—
He's standin' next his multilayer-collaged footlocker,
decked out with red mop hair, clown face red nose, multicolored pants,
a gold glittery vest & smiling face necktie & decaled baseball cap;
he perfected the craft of balloon twisting, whatever your fancy,
   he'll make a facsimile—
               Mr. Twister claimed he had no teacher,
learned it all on his own & did it his way,
   but, as he would say,
      Love, luck, & lots of coin,
      are a street performer's blessing,
         with a *honk honk* of his horn.

               And a Thread of memory is guiding me
through all the years of street performers on the Ave—
The hundreds of guitarists, violinists, flutists,
   & sax players,
          jazz ensembles,
   the Little Bit of Love singers
      ages 5 to 15
           showed up a season,
the Equal Time Sax Quartet on weekend afternoons;
last Labor Day a bass string wash tub thumper
   jammin' with some guitar player;
& the jugglers, comics, street poets, magicians,
   bubble makers...

       & a Thread is guiding me
for the performance that is a lifetime—

         One day I'm walking along
& these young guys walk by, I hear one ask of another,
 "Why did you dress up in drag? Were you confused by your girl?"
& others walk by, "Didn't you see her? She waved *at you,* Brad—"
& the missing-teeth man in blue jean jacket, been on this street for years,
as usual is talkin' aloud to himself,
 No napalm tonight...
       apparently reliving some fragment of memory,
& grungy youth are sittin' on the pavement lookin' pitiful, little sign askin'
 for money,
& a young woman is playin' a harp in a closed-for-the-day food kiosk alcove,
 singin' sweetly to ethereal angelic tones,
& on the cement edge of a planter box a gal guitarist sings,
 Spread your wings, you can fly...
& a Hare Krishna man with backpack paces one side the street,
 then the other,
    chantin' amidst tourists the endless Krishna mantra,
 starin' ahead,
     noninteractive,
& one afternoon Jeffrey the Hemp Poet & I were talkin',
 suddenly his eyes focused & followed four identical surf-&-sand girls
  walking along shoulder to shoulder,
& lesbian couples talk & smile, walkin' along nonchalant hand-in-hand,
& even on a chilly night I see a man standin' on the corner
next New Leaf Market beatin' a bongo, chantin'
 Santa Cruz, Santa Cruz, over & over
   & he sends out a howl *Aaahhhoooooo...*
& the spray paint artist Saturday nights sets up in front of Graphix,
his face hidden behind a double-barreled protective mask
quietly workin' ignorin' the audience always gathered,
a little boom box background music playin',
his works spread out for all to view—
these, like, extraordinarily otherworldly,
idealized, tropic splendorous of landscapes...

      And so I'm still sittin' havin' a coffee
at the Coffee Roasting Company, a woman in a long wool coat,
green parrot on her shoulder, sits next table over from me,
& what a range, like incredible, the voice of that parrot,
accosting people as they stroll along & wonder *What the heck?*
  Where did that come from?

       And I remember the man
—what was his name?—he had to have a name—
but let's just say he was the Starin'-at-the-Sun-Man—
20 years ago he used to stand on one of the corners of the ol' Mall,
  he'd stand there & just point & stare at the Sun,
    his mouth movin' like chompin' on somethin';
he looked like some long-bearded Hindu guru went crazed,
  just pointin' & starin', feedin' his eyes
    on the beautiful brilliance of the Sun.
        Vaguely I remember
he was murdered, pushed off a nearby bridge.
—It was the trolls did it, as some locals called the homeless
  who lived down by the bridge.
     And I remember another man,
he was the Man-Who-Paced—
he'd pace the ol' Mall always starin' at the pavement
both arms flailing, always swatting at imaginary somethings...

        And of course
we are descended upon by all the tourists & out-of-towners;
  & of course this is a student town—
everywhere you go, you find students, students,
  & more students
    —high school, Cabrillo College, but especially UCSC
     Like, dude, this has gotten to be quite the university town—
& there're all the street people, punkers, retro stylers,
  Christians passin' out their Jesus Saves leaflets
    —sometimes a group gathers with guitars
     & sings songs of Savior Jesus.

                              And I knew locals
who avoided the ol' Mall, who couldn't stand all the weirdness
     & the faces of the homeless,
'specially after Reagan cut social services back in the 80s
& the floodgates of mental institutions were thrown wide open
          —Saint Silicon years ago called The Cruz
               the largest open air asylum in the country.
And to me what a privilege it is
                         to live here
in such a multiple mini-world community
—or call it, if you wish, social/cultural diversity—
     the inner subterranean worlds allowed here
          —comparatively,
               to the majority of the country—
their 3rd-dimensional space-time expression,
               which is the richness of soul
                         we so much need

(—repression, I believe, is the original human madness—)

                    for it is here the Goddess
          liberates
     —& so let us honor the Goddess—

& let us share & reveal ourselves freely & openly,
     & do it with heart
               —& with Art.

                         Walkin' along now,
I stop to hear the dark moustache accordionist playin',
our getting-to-be-well-known Julio, The Great Morgani—
Some other guy, tipsy, moments before latched onto him,
                    & this guy's pudgy, a white moustache,
& is spoutin' somethin' Italian,
     O Mama Mia...Pizza Pie...
                         'bout all I can make out,
          & he snags a woman walkin' by
& they start dancin' to one of Julio's numbers
                    like gypsies of the street—

Aahhhh, he is in heaven, emoting melodious romance in Italian,
    they are this moment the scene—
And as the music ends, she plants a kiss on his cheek,
  & his surprise is like *Wow!*
& just as he hopes for more, she mentions a husband,
  & must go, & says
      Chaio—
And so perhaps this once only,
he would dance this one & only dance
       with her...

       And I'm rememberin'
the Cooper House, a Cruz historic building
brought down by the wrecking ball, so soon after the Quake—
The Crepe Place was in there then,
  & there was a bar—don't remember the name—,
  with light jazz a daily fare by a group name of Warmth
      playin' for customers outside
sittin' round tables, CinZano umbrellas shadin' 'em,
& people would stop & watch from the sidewalk & get to dancin',
  like Gypsy Rose would do, dancing there,
    on the sidewalk,
      & I knew a nurse from the hospital
    used to dance there too,
      on the sidewalk,
& it was one late summer sultry kickback evening
I sat there with Teresa & her beau
  toastin' drinks & sharin' feelin's,
     & it was such a romantic affair
    I had goin' with The Cruz,
  & this epiphany came to me,
  Why are we here?
I swooned on lavender air so gorgeous—
  We are here to create legends.

   And Psyche, master Thread maker
  & weaver of the Way,
     shows me
  my way—

                      And there she is,
lookin' all the part of the femme fatale,
standin' tall in tight black slacks, black glasses & a cap,
    sleeveless, bright red lips,
strummin' her guitar right here on the Ave—
She's singin',
        Let's go downtown,
        Let's go downtown tonight...

1999

Night Cruz'n Pacific Avenue

And on these balmy September Labor Day weekend evenings,
    the full Moon rising,
a great convergence of human desire plays out on Pacific Ave
as she on guitar one day would sing,
    Let's go downtown,
    Let's go downtown tonight...

                                  And so,
as if instinctively, as if a type of soul gravity works
at the heart of the city, a world of desire converges, & the parade
that began as day flourished up & down our main street Ave
now feels the flush of dusk—
                              And so inviting
the lure of lights like stars strung, in tree
after tree after tree, all the sparkles that run their branches—
how they glamour both sides the Avenue block by block
                              of the post-Quake Cruz.
All of desire's actors will attempt to play out their repertoires here—
Swarms of youth, the dating crowd, out-on-the-night couples,
    backpackers & restaurant goers,
street people & performers, the just regulars & loner guys cruz'n
tourists & over-the-summit Silicon Valley out-of-towners,
& a group of Aussies with camcorder are interviewing locals
    to take back Down Under
            —they sort'a grab me walkin' by—,
& Tom the Magic Man is set up as usual in front of GAP
& reels in the fishes who take the bait of fast talkin' suggestibility—
He dazzles them, as usual; they always walk away wonderin'
    how such magic is done.
                                And nearby,
a downtown regular sometimes also guitar bizarro
    —I've seen him for years—
is kneeled on the pavement with two puppets male & female,
brings his own cassette player music & has 'em dance all clunky-like
& perform these little improvisational skits trying to garner attention—
They're talkin' 'bout coffee, the habit, comparin' different local
    establishments,

                                           & hot spot most evenings
                         definitely is Santa Cruz Coffee Roasting Co.,
mobbed with groups of mid-to-late teens, twenty-somethings,
just hangin' out in front sippin' their to-go coffee & espresso drinks,
lightin' up cigarettes, talkin' like what scene they'll hit later,
& brash Starbucks moved in a direct shot across the street,
not so many hangin' out there; but these little groups, though,
face off
     both sides the street
                between which
                        cars cruise,
                blarin' hip hop or punk rock,
with guys checkin' out the babes in their showoff tight jeans
& short tight skirts & looks of O so cool,
                   you wonder where desire will lead
             this night—
                         And one evening
4 a cappella singers set up microphones & a speaker
in the outside Starbucks patio givin' a performance
attractin' more of the passin' sidewalk gawkers,
& course there's a mob in front of, mingling in with,
the lines at the giant marquee Santa Cruz Cinema 9 lookin' more like
    Wilshire Boulevard LA,
& traffic goes in & out Blockbuster Music next door on the corner,
& Mike the Bubble Gique would be here too, on-the-corner maker
of bubbles huge enough to even impress Gargantua,
      but he's this weekend at Burning Man in Nevada,
& across the way street hippies lounge on the pavement
     along a red, plastic-lined chain link fence
          hidin' where the ol' landmark Cooper House used to be,
snubbing a silly ordinance 'bout loitering—
      Three police officers happen by,
                   ask questions,
                         but nothing further;
on Saturday a sax player will be there doin' his gig.
                         And I gaze up
& see the full Moon hangin' expectantly in clear sky above,
    reminder of some origin of desire,

& a short distance away the accordionist The Great Morgani,
    playin' almost every evening in front of Shen's Gallery,
          swings to a snappy polka number—
He's always in a different outfit,
tonight in white dress shirt with yellow sparkling beret,
last night in his glittery East European harlequin sleeves
    with black vest & black Zorro hat,
          always an audience of a handful standin' around
    & sittin' on benches nearby
          —he'll play requests for those who ask
      & sometimes he gets 'em dancin',
as a couple dances now
          to a slow romantic number.

        And down by Costa Brava,
a live stompin' music restaurant,
a couple are standin' & playin' guitars singin',
    Oh baby, baby, it's a wild world...
              & next door
people are lined up to make the trip up the steps
to Rosie McCann's Irish Pub, they got the live loud sound too
    & stompin' crowd,
& guys up & down the Ave sit on the edges of cement planter boxes
    alone or with friends
          fingerin' their guitars
              —what is *their* desire?—,
& a hippy guy walks by lookin' lost in the throng,
there's a sign hangin' from his neck, simply says "Tarot,"
& local poet Bert Glick is always cruz'n through, always focused
    straight ahead, apparently never sees me.
And how many stand in circles & parade in waves, cruz'n the scene
in their baseball caps, oversized t-shirts & baggy pants,
    or tattered jeans & tie-dyed shirts,
while tourists stroll casually on the decks of The Cruz
in their fresh-laundered shorts & Birkenstock sandals...
          And so many businesses stay open late—
East Meets West shares door with Natural Treasures,
Eclectix, naughty-filled Camouflage, RAGE
    (meaning Recycled American Garment Exchange),

Pacific Wave, Many Hands Gallery, the ID Building
    (meaning Integrand Design),
Bookshop Santa Cruz with Georgianna's in front, another café
    to hang out at,
& someone there is playin' violin, tomorrow, it'll be guitar,
& almost directly across the street is Super Crown Books
with its "Going Out Of Business" banner
—committed the arrogance of hubris on The Cruz,
    now everything is on sale.
And even a place like Bunny's Shoes is open late.

                      And a new gay bar
Club Dakota has its little happenin' hot scene
next where Tom has staked out his stage in front of GAP
with new people always gathered around, spillin' over—
    the show once again goes on.
Peet's Coffee & Tea, another alternative, will get its share
    of the crowd,
& at the quiet Town Clock end of the main Pacific drag so, too,
Espresso Royale Caffe (the old Lulu Carpenter's, popular bar
    of pre-Quake days),
& Pacific Avenue Pizza & Grille is servin' till 11:00
    & at the opposite end the Ave
        Pizza My Heart, with packed outside tables,
            —it's the local favorite & a long-established joint—,
            also stays open for the late-night bite,
& the B of A Versateller is hit up over and over for fast cash,
& Pacific Cookie Co. you see how it's starkly well lit with displays
    of big cookie sweets,
& the old classic Del Mar Theatre you see is all lit up
    but no longer the crowds of yesteryear,
              & Marini's mint-green-lit name overhead
hints of its bright sparkling glass counters of candies & ice cream;
& New Leaf Market in the old big bank building corner of Soquel
—it's so bright-looking inside—its customers come & go till 9.
                      And there's a jam
at the corner down from Palookaville where punk rock new wavers
are playin' loud way loud, you can hear 'em poundin' thru the wall,
& the sidewalk crowd is waitin' to get in, tryin' to get in
    —tickets all sold—,

so they're just hangin' out beside the big road buses,
apparently the place to be—for now—wherever desire may lead—,
& of course The Catalyst—ol' Cruz landmark, I knew it well years ago—
draws its share of the nightclub going—for years its heyday glory days
    were guaranteed every Friday & Saturday night,
& Logos Used Books is browser's magnet & popular thoroughfare
    —a rendezvous point every day for so many here—,
& next door is Double Rainbow Cafe with its neon ice cream cone
    & neon coffee cup,
                I never yet stepped into,
& parked in front of the Sockshop another door down
a most remarkable car I spot, an art car—an old BMW—
of incredible detail, as it's utterly covered with baubles
    & figurines & all kinds of whatever,
of which to attempt to describe I could not do justice to,
    not here, not at this moment.
People can't help but stare, some sittin' on a bench nearby;
& I sit, take some notes, & walk circles around it,
& suddenly the owner walks up & wonders of my interest—
She's a friendly ol' tie-dyed hippy goin' way back.

                And on this Sunday
after the crowds have gone, as I sit & watch,
here, at a Coffee Roasting Co. outside table,
reflecting on The Cruz, how it all happened this weekend,
a group is gathered round another table intent on netting
    those still searchin' passin' by,
talkin' 'bout dancin' to the Spirit, I hear mention of Jesus,
    must be some Christian group.

                    And I reflect
that amidst all this convergence of human desire
stands in utter silence a huge structure
sharing the other corner of Soquel 'bout 7 stories tall,
an absolutely dark skeleton of a building going up
    everyone just walks by
thru this red painted plywood & scaffolding walkway
    running alongside,
another rebirth from the ground up of our Quake
    9 years ago—

                              As I reflect,
I am reminded of the enormously huge darkness
    within our Bay—
                              I think of all
the convergence of energy & desire,
of human intention & dreaming & planning,
round the beautiful shores of our Bay of Monterey.

                              I reflect
how desire draws them all to this place,
as desire draws everyone everywhere at all times
    to some rendezvous.
                    Desire—
    the universal motivator,
    but then—
              What then?
Do they find satisfaction? That object of desire?
Or is it frustration of one kind or another?
    Or is there something more?
For as the parade began, the parade must end.

As I left the scene on a previous evening
—whether Friday or Saturday, I can't remember—,
    as I turned a corner,
I saw this hippie couple quietly eating a pizza out of a box
on the pavement beside a building whose facade column
    hid them from the fray.

    Desire—
comes as simple as eat & survive,
but let us hope there is something more—
    What then?
There is Vision, revealing a whole other Story to tell,
to take desire on a whole other Cruz.

September 1998

The Avenue is Empty

                          Three of us
are walking down Pacific Avenue
on this relatively pleasant late spring, nearing sunset
    of an evening,
& we have never seen anything like this—
The avenue is empty—we look down the sidewalk
& block after block there is scarcely a soul to be seen.
Pacific should be alive, teeming, with streams of people—
Pacific Ave, the very heart of The Cruz—pulsing arteries
of people should be flowing up & down both sides the street,
but it's the COVID-19, the tiny, tiny, invisible, virus,
the Virus, that the mainstream narrative tells us we should be
afraid of, as we are all potential carriers of its death-making
intent, still has everyone keeping away.
                              Yes, a few crazies
—so noticeable now, how they stand out—
are cruising along, sidewise looking, uttering monologues
of their own…& here & there, we spot a person or two
patronizing one of the open, take-out restaurants,
or a shop or two, with restrictions, that do have open doors.
Almost literally, though, we look down the long avenue
of sidewalk & no one, for long moments there is no one;
    it is an eerie, utter silent zone—
It appears we are in some tunnel of the Underworld
—*where exactly are we?* we wonder aloud—
yet here we are, right in the heart of The Cruz…
And there has not been a cop in sight—
No sign of any police our whole time in town.
But three of us sat on a bench this evening
& enjoyed our delicious—it's birthday Steve today—
    Laili dinner take-out…

May 31, 2020

Pacific Avenue Alive Again

       It's a Sunday
& it's so good to see the life
of Pacific Avenue thriving again—
Last spring saw the COVID-induced
death of the avenue—you would find
but few souls out sauntering along last spring,
most businesses had shut their doors—,
but summer brought back life to the heart
of The Cruz again.
        I've come into town today
& am strolling along the avenue & so many people
are out strolling along too…businesses are open,
though a number, unfortunately, have not
  survived…
       Many restaurants you find open—
One whole block between Cathcart & Lincoln
is closed off to vehicles; instead, tables are set up
for outside eating as never before, in front
the restaurants & along the sidewalk…
Kianti's Pizza & Pasta Bar on the corner
  with three fire towers flaming…
High Tide Poke Shop, HOM Korean Kitchen,
  SNAP Taco…
And on the opposite side the Ave
Melo Melo Kava Bar, with its two fire towers,
Mission Hill Coffee & Creamery & Five Guys burgers…
A black guy on sax, a white guy on guitar
are playing & singing on the curb & street to all—
They get rounds & rounds of applause.

      Around the corner,
down Cathcart, barricaded along the street
outside seating has taken over the sidewalk
in front of Hula's Island Grill, Tiki Room, & Lupulo—
That had already been popular along there
for eating & drinking wine for sometime
since at least last year.

                        I enjoyed hearing
four different groupings of musicians
along the avenue this afternoon—
At the prominent corner in front of
O'Neill Surf Shop was also a quartet of musicians
—clarinet, bass, guitar, drums—
playing to people who always gather
for the music there…& some were dancing.
A short distance away, Robert Perala who I know
was on guitar & another guitarist was with him—
They were strumming away & singing
    a variety of songs…

So good to see the life of Pacific Avenue
    had come back…
so good to see that people had come back…

October 4, 2020

Santa Cruz the Bubble

They say people here live in a bubble,
that Santa Cruz exists in its own dream world,
an illusory of a beautiful bubble dream world,
a seducing all over casualness of attitude
    you find so often makes for
        this fog-brained, fuzzy of a kind'a whatever,
           hangin' loose-like way of perception—
A haven they say Santa Cruz is of the weird
    & the wacky,
a never-wanna-grow-up land of Peter Pans
the rest of the adult country, *the real world*, as they say,
    loves to poke fun of—
Oh, Santa Cruz—weird is the word, you know,
a notoriously laid-back, surfin' dude town,
lots of your squishy soft, do-gooder, progressive liberals
& time-warped flower children left over from the Sixties...

But there is so much more about The Cruz,
however its shimmering unreality of bubble
people here might give all the impression of living in.
There is more, there is something quite other,
something revelatory you had not expected,
    happening here—

           Enter the bubble
& you'll find a swirl of a vortex in it,
a fitful creativity churning in the cauldron
    of the bubble—
        There's new life astir
in the swirl of this vortex,
in the fitful creativity churning & churning
    in the cauldron
        of the bubble,

an emerging divine shining presence
        out here on the continent's edge,
where Goddess of this place, our Bay of Monterey,
    is all so apparent in Her splendor,
      where, within the bubble
—hidden to the pundits of everyday worldliness—,
our Goddess is giving birth to the Unheard-of,
to burst through from inside the bubble—
It is the coming-to-us from out of the Pacific
    of the future's Golden Child.

December 2004

Santa Cruz *The Cruz*

> *It's the easy Cruz'n rhythm*
> *you'll find*
>   *as I have found—*
>
> *It's the ever-changing rhythm*
> *of surprise*
>   *surf is*

A state of mind they say of this place The Cruz—
Like, it's *The Cruz*, the beautiful Cruz, the easy livin', laid back,
trippin' along whatever you wanna be Cruz, like, nowhere else.

          The Cruz—
Like, all you have'ta do is go out
and experience it for yourself & you'll know why—
                  Go out & stand upon a bluff
and gaze upon the Sun-bright beaches goin' round the Bay
    & you'll get the feel alright,
it's as gorgeous of a diamond-scintillating Goddess coast
    as you will ever find.
They know who come streaming & streaming in—
        And they *do* come, down Ocean Street, to play the day
at the amusement-packed, the one-&-only of the West Coast,
Beach Boardwalk & Casino Fun Center—inside Cocoanut Grove—,
their crazy loud & lights galore of rides & games & arcades
    all these crowds of summertime
                converge upon;
and they come to hit the tourist shops & restaurants of the wharf,
    to beach blanket the sands, like, just catchin' the rays;
        at the edge of the sea, imagine, all the picnickers
           & beachgoers;
            & they gather round evening fire pits;
    or you see the loners just saunterin' the strand,
        as surfer dudes are out cruzin' a ride on the big ones
            curlin' in at Steamer Lane
              —it's big time surfer town, the original Surf City—,

Lighthouse Point there on the rock torn edge of the world
the waves & waves & waves of the great Pacific
    will pound & pound upon—
                                Oh, but She calms
the ferociousness of the incoming open Sea,
the Bay waters of autumn their turquoise sheen is utter tranquility,
and brilliant the pallets of sunset cloud, mesmerizing all who stand in awe
    upon the bluffs of The Cruz—
The Sun goes down & there's somethin' about the Pacific horizon.

                  The mudslide rains
of winter gray will pour & pour down,
but minstrels have set up & make music just inside from the rain,
the shiny wet colors outside all so rich, such richness of the shiny greens,
    the flowers—
In the winter, still flowers; in January, already acacias are blooming,
    already the beginning of the long rise of spring...

                                  The Cruz—
Where heavy, coastal curtains of fog, how they get pulled in
after the heat of days, the sudden summertime surprising chill,
yet desire-inspiring the warmth you find of the strangely
    illuminated nights;
and you will find the mellow of Sun-filled summery-like days
    right smack in the middle of winter days.
                              You will see then
the Santa Lucia Mountains standin' out clear & bold
    other side the Bay,
legendary Big Sur pointing giants beyond Monterey.
And you are dreamin' the dream you are here—
    such beauty is equal to any.

                          Seems—yes—the quiet
redwood mountains & the Bay of an Ocean surrounding
circumscribe a realm of always-to-the-newcomer paradise—
Oh, and such a life-is-so-good, isn't it, to be cruzin' like this,
sippin' on your glass'a primo California wine or a piña colada
gazin' out the big harbor restaurant windows
    watchin' the sailing yachts come & go
            —every Wednesday it's the sailing regatta—;

     or you're scannin' the sands of the bikini-clad below,
or you're loungin' with a fruit combo smoothie out on some palm patio,
or you hang out hours chatting or people watchin' at some one among
  so many cafés—
          Pacific Avenue
inside the Vortex The Cruz swirls & swirls its currents
of people pulled in—from all over the world they get pulled in,
always the tourists & new arrivals, the students & visitors marooned,
  always you find the soul-searching wanderers
& those just passing through, always the just-out-of-towners
& locals who come out cruzin' on the Ave just about every day—
Impressions gather of this ongoing promenade up & down the Ave,
the yearlong cruzin' bloomin' diverse panoply of persons—
of course the street performers famous of the Ave—
you'll hear the music, the beat, the poets recite,
watch artists of bubbles & balloons,
of mime & costume,
    oh, the weirdness & wackiness,
  you'll see it all,
       & all just cruzin' bein' freely who they are.
As young skateboarders push off like surfin' the slope of streets
  throughout The Cruz.
Like, it's as cool & as casual as, *What's happenin', dude?*
  Like, whatever, *just bein'*—

         The Cruz—
As pelicans cruise along just above the rollin' surf,
as the cormorants gather upon the sea-stained stacks
and gulls you see turn & turn like easy in the wind,
as shearwaters by the thousands will thousands of miles
  come to feast,
as seals & sea lions sun on the flat sea rocks, sleep under the wharf,
as sea otters—look out among the kelp bed blades—you'll see 'em
  rollin' & poppin' up in the canopy of blades,
    & whales you might catch sight of off in the distance,
as sandpipers run the tongues of beached wave,
and stately egrets & herons stalk in the rivers & marshes & lagoons,
as the mockingbirds of spring will sing crazily here, all night.

As the monarchs of wintertime flit & sail all about town,
and return at evening chill to the sheltering eucalyptus
    of Natural Bridges—
                                      People gaze up
into the fluttering orange & black clusters of them,
a marvelous sight among cruzin' sights—
                      Marvelous, all of them.

                     Oh, you'll hear
the drummin' circles out on the beaches
and see all the strollin', ocean-transfixed persons out on the cliffs
    of West Cliff,
and the endless sands of dreaming you'll find southward the Bay—
Even in later autumn the big family spread Thanksgiving feasts
you find under the canopy of tables at Seacliff Beach—
Or mingle among the summer leisurely on the tourist-happy,
picture-perfect Esplanade walk of Capitola-by-the-Sea;
                      or inside the Vortex Pacific Ave,
lose yourself as multi-thousands swirl in mass together
into the annual mad cauldron of Halloween—
                                      The cruzin' rhythm
playin' upon evening's encircling pink & lavender horizon
    you're sure to get caught up in,
like all the wild & wonderful, livin' freely of abundant living things
interconnected as the rich biodiversity of place so precious
    of this coast.

We will always when we hear mention of *Santa Cruz*
remember how this was the unparalleled beautiful state of mind,
    The Cruz.

December 2006/2007

This Cruz

This Cruz is such a groove,
like it likes itself so much—ya know?
Youth poppin' everywhere, multi-mini-worlds
    of a swirlin' hip town,
streamin' students & searchin' souls flock in
from all over places,
                you see 'em,
                          eyes, like, look around—
      Like, it's just too cool, dude—
Yeah, it's college & university party town alright,
      laid back surfin'/skateboarder/tourist-trippin' town—
                Like, it's The Cruz, man.
And they hang out/study hours in packed chatter-filled cafés
    —it's, like, ultimate café town—,
& hot groups & performers are hittin' the clubs & bars,
there're all kinds'a art & theatre & dance groups, performance artists,
alternative/cutting edge of whatever you might imagine,
all kinds'a classes, all kinds'a whatever little study groups
& discussion groups, support groups, whatever kind'a groups,
    it's, like, ultimate *whatever* town—
                        And there's
downtown of a vortex Pacific Ave,
        its street life like a constant happenin' scene,
it, like, all seems to be happenin' here, always so much to take in,
                          all packed in so tight—
Book & music stores, art galleries, films foreign & artsy,
    big Hollywood-like Cinema 9,
like restaurants every block ta spoil ya,
                espresso drinks every corner,
    cool shops all kinds'a stuff,
& of course the Beach Boardwalk a West Coast original,
    an Americana classic—

There're hiking trails
in meditative-inspiring, redwood-hushed mountains,
      miles of sand ta wander & get lost on,
 & West Cliff always so pretty postcard posed;
like this Cruz is saturated, it's, like, almost too much,
  creative energies movin' like constant everywhere,
    little vortices of subculture ta make ya crazy
      with so much.
And there're plenty who take this Cruz—at least for a while—,
and some—well, they get pulled in completely
& get strung out on a lifetime of Cruz'n—
  I've seen 'em,
    I'm probably one.

But there is a question, to always ask,
no matter how too cool it all is—
What this town asks,
  what any town asks,
    is,
 What will you assimilate of it?
What will you
   make new
     out of the essence
       of yourself?
 What will you give back?

Too much this always take & take,
  consume & drain—
What a place asks for
  is your contribution—
  What have you done, dude?
    What difference
      did your presence
         make?

February 2000

A Lotta Talk

There's a lotta talk spinnin' all over The Cruz,
a whole lotta talk goin' round circles of The Cruz—
There's a lotta drug-induced rappin' smoke-dreamin' talk,
    a lotta delusional makin'-it-big talk,
a lotta culture junkie know-it-all name-droppin' talk,
a lotta hip New Age vibrational glamour & sage-smudgin'
    & psychic energy talk,
a lotta holier-than-thou politically correct talk,
    a lotta the usual drinkin' nightclubbin' talk—
There's a lotta jivin' peddled on the streets of The Cruz,
a lotta big plans talked in the cafés of The Cruz,
    a lotta manic ambition & no fruition,
there's a lotta promisin' made in the fog here on The Cruz
& very little in proportion
                is ever done
                        or accomplished—

She is maker of Neptune illusion,
She is easy talkin' temptation,
She is Oh so cool sittin' round laid back goin' nowhere
    but a whole lotta talk—
So little finds its way to manifestation for the Cruz'n
    who so dislike the labor of Saturn—
It's, like, She's gotcha, if that's how you want Her,
    but a whole lotta talk.
                    Otherwise—
The talkin' tongue must have roots,
    roots that go down,
deep as the canyon, as She is deep,
when you truly do find Her,
                out there,
                    in the Bay.

October 2000

An Old Illusion

I remember when I was new in The Cruz late 70s
there were those of us newcomers
—always there are those of us newcomers—
who fostered among ourselves
the illusion
        this was a place
                where we could be
    all one together community,
            where indeed
we could all
        get to know one another,
somehow live
      as a mutually supportive,
extended kind'a family—
      Of course the "Establishment" here,
& certain cliques of local culture
            —you had'da be in,
   or else—,
             didn't think so,
& I suppose we were naïve
           to think so—
    By 1980 overnight
           seemed the illusion
    was dashed.
It was apparent the new wave youth
who swarmed into town that year
    Who were they? Where did they all come from?
           had other agendas—

—Like, dude, you gotta realize
           this is a transient town,
  a UC town,
like of course they're comin' & goin' all the time—
    students, tourists, searchin' souls just cruz'n awhile,

                        & yuppies
                                    don't care for nothin'
                            but makin' money & buyin' up things,
            gettin' their heels
                        dug in.

—Yeah, the Reagan Neptune-in-Capricorn years,
            saw the glamorization of wealth & success,

    besides,
            this town's gotten too big
                    for any old Sixties community sense,
                            it's just
                    too diverse,
                                too much happenin',
        you're just part of
                    at best
                            a mini-world here—

So community is a Vision
hovering some distance
from the hand's awkward grasp...
but the poet tries
    nonetheless
to make real
in some way
such a needful
            Illusion.

February 2000

Find Yourself a Vision

From the university upon a hill,
spread broad & blue & curved before me,
the open body of the Bay, a beautiful Vision to gaze upon.
And all The Cruz is spread before me, a patterned story fabric
of trees woven, all the bushy greenery, buildings & houses,
telling of grids of streets laid out, implying a narrative
    that is the life of a city;
& there are lovely fields & meadows I see,
the distant wharf & Dream Inn, a strip visible of Highway 1
    I see;
& woven into this vision, there is more—
Interpenetrating all is the living Fabric
    that cannot be seen
                but with other eyes.

                            To the distant left,
the lazy backbone of mountain of green & darker green
    half circling The Cruz;
there, prominent, the dark Eye of Loma Prieta.
And sprinkled across Her pale blue flesh, little white sails
    & comet tails of motor boats,
& across the body of the Bay, through pale haze & cloud,
    the ghostly peaks above Monterey—
And I have seen the Sun burn upon the waters of the Bay.

    It is a potent Vision. But still, only the surface.

    Once, I stood upon
                Twin Lakes Beach with a friend
    —I was still new in The Cruz then—;
we talked of others, how fateful it was that so many
had found their way here, & how many would settle here
& attempt to fulfill a destiny woven into this land,
a land abundant with such desire & such promise—

      How many come with some dream?
        How many are able to fulfill it?

Tremendous forces, elemental, primordial, have shaped this land;
   and still latent, always latent,
and always ready on some smaller human scale to destroy or create;
   I know, I have seen it—
           She is the living memory of it.
For She will desire you & press up close to you
   & would think to keep you,
       only to deceive & destroy you, gullible you.
     Or—if you are lucky, if you are prepared,
  She will consider you of some use.
     —To make a child by.
    Born of this land.

Who would survive this place, this advice:
   Prepare yourself.
Find yourself a Vision, for only a Vision can save you,
the human equal to
         Mountain, Ocean, Sun.

UC Santa Cruz
June 1998

The Poet-Who-Walks

I am *The-Poet-Who-Walks-the-Streets*—
Perhaps you've seen me out walkin' the streets
    of The Cruz,
my writing pad craddled in the crook of my arm—
You might have seen me sometime out on West Cliff
    or East Cliff,
or saunterin' down Seabright or cruz'n Pacific Ave
—where I now do my street performin' routine—,
or perhaps you've seen me out walkin' Ocean, Water,
    or Soquel,
               Branciforte or Morrissey,
Mission Street or Broadway, California
    or Dakota;
you might have caught me at one time headin' down
    Poplar
            or when I lived on Bay—
Been doin' it now over 20 years on The Cruz,
I always find myself out walking again with paper & pen,
as walking is a centering in the midst of the whirl
of events & change of always so much these days
    happening—

            To speak of place firsthand,
you must get out & walk—
You must observe, listen, smell, absorb
through every pore of your body
    the feel of atmosphere,
        all the impressions comin' in,
            and yes, return again
    & again,
to where you once were & once walked
when called to weave the Threads of place
    into a tapestry complete,
                     as tonight,
I walk up Walnut Street from Pacific,
there is a staircase
    other side of Chestnut,

                    up the ridge there,
I used to climb to the westside,
          was 16 or more years ago—
Has it been that long?

                    So I return
to climb these steps once again,
          & I encounter no one,
the neighborhood above is so quiet here,
                    only the crickets I hear
          & smell of jasmine so prominent,
as if this one little nook in all the changin' world
has been crystallized out in the currents of time—
And I look out over the rooftop lights
     of midtown
& the bright twinkling lights
          of no fog clear sky—

                    And those singular evergreens
a distance away so tall
               are still conversing
as a woman I once knew
          once told me
she heard them converse,
                         there,
               in the air,
                         above it all.

               Yes,
this is how it's done,
the weaving of a Story,
the birthing process of Mythos
The-Poet-Who-Walks-the-Streets
     is called
          by the Word
               to tell…

August 2000

Café Cruz'n

On this Cruz you won't find a more classic poet
of café life than this café lovin' poet who's been Cruz'n
since the pre-Quake pre-Café Zinho days of Caffé Pergolesi—
It was in the Courtyard behind the Bookshop day after day
I'd hang out at Pergolesi in my early strugglin' writer days
& contend with the young, Postmodern, student
intellectuals there, workin' on my great unfinished
Santa Cruz novel *Psyche/Aphrodite*...

      & then opened
Café Domenica in the old Dr. Miller's Building
where the blastin' loud punker crowd Pergolesi
  you find located today
    (the ol' Pergolesi switched ownership,
     became Café Zinho in the Courtyard,
      while Domenica switched & became Pergolesi;
      that was the pre-Quake 80s)
& the once Café Caméléon on Front Street
  (where So Say We & dance studio 418 you find today)
    I'd hang out there too, a rather youth exclusive
     kind'a decadent street life scene
—they dressed like somethin' out of a Mad Max movie wildly eccentric
  in those late 80s days—,
that's where I did my solo 2 ½ hour reading "Becoming Visible Again,"
& St. Silicon & I & others also performed a couple shows there,

       & I remember
I used to frequent Mr. Toots early-mid 80s afternoons,
I would ride a bus out to Toots in Capitola to write
& sat with many a woman over the years there takin' in
the balcony view of little Italy by-the-Sea,

    & summertime early 90s afternoons
  I liked the Jahva House,
 a high rafter of an airy place, on Union,
you can see was once a big shop or warehouse,
with seemingly its own internal weather—

                              blackbirds would fly in
the wide opened wall, peruse the floor what they might find;
school year it was always packed with students, no place to sit,
but cubbyhole Caffé Bené's round the corner,
     if you needed a quick to-go...

                    Or, if I'm on the westside,
rare occasions I stop in at the back-in-the-corner
of the shopping plaza there kind'a hidden away Westside Coffee,
or sometimes with a friend or two I hit—always seems busy—
     Caffe Royale
               on north end of Pacific Ave,
its classy décor still the look of the bar Lulu Carpenter's it once was
(—& now, Year 2000, still a café, but the name Lulu Carpenter's it is
          once again—)

                    or, if I'm into watchin' the parade
on Pacific, it's Santa Cruz Coffee Roasting Company,
changed its interior literally overnight recently—instead of tables,
now it's wooden booths & cushioned seats,
                         & the people parade
is always chargin' through, as they come in right off the Ave—
(There is always of course a Starbucks & Peet's on the Ave,
     if you choose.)

                    & my usual stop before work in Aptos
is Trout Gulch Coffee, choose from bagels, breakfast burritos,
or somethin' sweet;
          they all know me there now, the gals all friendly,
               & I always manage to squeeze in a few lines
          before showing up the road
                         at herbalist Paul's,

                    & of course my absolute favorite café
goin' on 3 years now into the New Millennium
—you'll find me almost every evening after work Monday thru Friday
     at this on-my-way-home stop—,

                              55

it's The Ugly Mug Coffeehouse downtown Soquel, a so cozy
    & comfy café,
the just right, perfect atmosphere café, also serves delicious gelato,
almost always tables are available, though some evenings
    it's student packed,
        with Cabrillo College up the road a ways,
            oh, there's some from the university too,
or, on occasional performance nights, it gets blastin',
    & there's scarcely a seat at all;
last year I led little discussions on the New Age here—
    Oh, I'm always gravitating to The Mug
whenever I'm aimless, go thru phases like I'm here 7 days a week,
hot beach summertime afternoons sometimes I'm the only soul
    in the place,
& naturally everyone here knows me,
            I have to be one of the all time regulars,

        & I like Java Junction,
    eastside The Cruz,
to look out its bright window patio, to the pumpin' hip music;
it's not all that far from the cliffs, end of Seabright,
a short hop & I can go & park & gaze upon
    our Goddess,
        our beautiful Bay of Monterey,
or, get out & take a walk down upon the sands...

       & still I frequent Pergolesi,
like to show up there occasionally
    —seems the right place—
        in a cross-dress mode,
& there's the small White Raven cozy up in Felton
    now that I've moved here,
& Rhonda introduced me to Abouché in Scotts Valley
—another possible stop as I make my way home,
    if I happen to take that route now—
wasn't even aware it's been there awhile,

          & when I was still up late & goin',
the best all-night coffee in town,
yes, it was the WashRock laundry, downtown,
next the Saturn…
                (it's closed down now—)

And so it goes—
We all must find a place where inspiration
    will flow.
And so I weave into my Story—
Cafés of The Cruz are, like, where I go…

February 2000

Survival Mode

like enough, enough, it's just too much already,
it's like another just gettin' by, scrapin' by, barely makin' it story,
such a constant struggle this town, O life is so good—
rents too high, jobs don't pay, housing is a scramble, UC talkin' 'bout
    pullin' in more students,
30-Day Notices, owners wanna sell, owners wanna jack up the rent,
you moved in too many people,
       bumped from house to house for years,
                      like, it's movin' time again,
   first, last, deposit—
              Who has it?

it's like the low-end-just-survivin' don't belong here anymore

     Is that the blunt truth?

                              it's commonplace anymore,
adult shared housing you get burned out on the whole trip,
sleepin' on living room sofas, sleepin' in attics, garages, shacks out back,
behind the house a room not meant for livin', vans parked in front,
someone's always short on cash, *Can you wait till next week?*
utilities need to be paid, 48-Hour Notice, got turned off
    'cause someone didn't come through,
you're gettin' burned again, in every household
    there's a slacker—

Can we get the rent money together, folks?

workin' just to pay rent & bills—
    Is that what it comes down to?
       simply survivin'— ?
                   need to borrow again,
adult children wanna be taken care of,
petty arguments 'bout a couple dollars,

                the Gods-not-so-spiritual,
are they laughin' upstairs somewhere?
                         watchin' these humans
constant scammin' a few bucks
in the basement of evolution,

You have poverty consciousness

the favorite gibe thrown around
—easy for those with fat bank accounts to say—,

you're an arm's length from the street
    & who cares?
        Who is responsible?
            Who even wants to be responsible?

Those with money, of course, think nothin' of it—

   —You know, you should'a got in'ta high-tech
   when you had the chance...

The Secret Controllers of this world don't care,
superfluous people, to them, sprout up everywhere—
And so it goes, all the way down
                        the social ladder,
   we learn from grade one
              not to care

even the bottom feeders want others to care,
   do they care?
            —Resentment runs deep here

   Who cares?
            Nobody cares—
   Social services play
by the rules,
            lose out, if you don't.

Get on food stamps, panhandle, sleep in your car
—if you can get away with it—,
or, like you're flat out homeless,
                    while SSI is a favorite
          for some—
                    get on that & you think you're set,
     for a life, it turns out, predetermined,
               of extreme financial perpetual survival,

& up on the UC campus,
     professors talk arcane Derrida deconstruction,
          text gibberish
                    for the select & privileged few—
It's advanced Postmodern new Millennium
     living
          on USS S. Cruz...

January 2000

Tents

Night, it's chilly, light rainy, it's miserable to be outside—
Who would want to be outside on a night like this?

        What is that?
What is going on there?
You're driving by, Highway 1 at River St.,
& squeezed behind the Gateway Plaza & the highway,
up against the San Lorenzo levee—*what was that?*
    What mirage was that?
Tents? There must have been a hundred of them—
Tents, small, in neat rows, shiny wet, you could make out
    a few colors in the dark…
Tents—in this weather? And all this winter season?
How is it possible to live like that?
A whole tent encampment is out there,
in the night, in this inhospitable night, in the cold,
    in the rain—
Who are these people who can settle into such a night?
—The homeless. The Santa Cruz homeless.
    It's the homeless encampment,
    the so-called Tent City.

And Santa Cruz wants to do something about it—
Like, what? Where can these people go?
What is happening here, Santa Cruz?
And not only in Santa Cruz—
What is happening here, America?
America, how can this be? *You are*—
America the wealthy,
America the bountiful,
America the great,
America the moral leader,
America, protector
of its citizens—
Yes? No?

March 11, 2019

Parade into First Night

Through the crowd I drifted, probably some few thousand
were here by now, packed on the sidewalk & flowing into the corridor
    of Pacific Ave—
I felt the anticipation of this entire evening
    & wondered where I should stand & catch the parade;
       & amidst all the jostling for positions
   —people were pouring in from all directions—,
I decided curbside where the parade would in fact begin.
And so appropriate in the clear fading blue above
the two Goddesses appeared—
                    Crescent Moon
    & to the right a diagonal
              famous brightest Venus,
& the parallel rows both sides the Avenue of starry lit little trees
were like frail sails that held steady upon the swell of the thronging
sea;
    & all the kids, of all ages, were so eager—

        And this Cruz'n parade into First Night
had to be the oddest, quirkiest, funkiest,
incongruously eclectic troupe of whatever one could imagine
    putting together—
                   Little girl silver stars
danced before the tall, spindly-armed visage
    of the Sun God
who annually leads & is symbol of this whole affair,
its big broad golden face stopping momentarily here & there
    to shine its smile upon the crowd,
& was followed by an array of balancing monocyclists & stilt walkers,
then some bagpipe & drum club & Renaissance minstrels & dancers,
& then this Techno Light Man stepped forward, who, with hands
    motioning in front of him,
remote controlled some funny little mousy vehicle scurrying
    in advance of him,
& there were some robots crude made of boxes,
& the Art & Revolution group, some costumed as missiles,
    were goin' round with buckets askin' for money,

mocking military dollars for putting weapons in space,
& all kinds'a space aliens streamed by & waved to us,
    the gawking humans,
& another who-knows-what-it-was-supposed-to-be-kind'a vehicle
    sported along,
& there was a flying pig as *Pink Floyd* once sang
& assorted bizarre animals & butterfly-winged women,
& various color-lit insects & a very long, floppy-bodied serpent
    held up on poles by half a dozen paraders,
& big, dreadlocked Rasta heads bopped along,
people strode along with guitars, tambourines & cowbells,
    flutes & violins,
& young sprites waved these enormously long streamers
whose ends danced & snapped over the heads of the crowd,
& how many others were there in this mad mad parade
of impressions, I can't say,
        I simply cannot remember them all.

                So it ended;
but then the whole hyperenergetic evening
    was still to unfold—
How many thousands were still pouring in & gathering,
spawning a New Year's celebration of the arts,
performances happenin' in all kinds'a various locations
    all over downtown,
& all kinds'a whooping it up merrymaking & craziness,
all the ruckus youth, live bands, food stands, a block of art cars,
    the loud blarin' Elvis car,
        all goin' down on this First Night on the Ave—
Hour after hour passed of agitated & aimless & shifting currents
    of persons
        culminating as a huge crowd of how many more thousands
            at the Town Clock quarter to midnight,
      a huge video screen there & laser light show
that sent mirror ball reflected spots of the laser's neon lime green
    in swirling circles out over the streets & buildings
        & over the heads of the New Year's clamoring throng.
Loud shouts & howls & all kinds'a cacophonous blarin' noise-making
    went up
        as the clock struck twelve.

      And a toast I made:
This is it, folks, first night of the first, completed year
  of our New Millennium—it's 2001,
a New Age Odyssey such as history has never before
  witnessed.

     And a poet was here,
as a poet always should be,
to help celebrate in memory
     what
    in full embodiment
  had defined
   a time
    & a place.

January 2001

A New Years Day Tradition

A New Years Day tradition in Felton
continues at the home of Peggy Black, now its 17th year
    in the year 2017—
Three of us, Rhonda, Steve, & this is my 4th year,
come in about mid-afternoon—
                          Dozens & dozens,
some years a hundred—we've heard even two hundred—
people come & go all day long till late afternoon's fading of light.
A great many come especially for something soulfully personal.
Those who have been here know the implication;
the annual New Years Day ritual
    waits
           out the back door…

                            But first—
A potluck spread all around the kitchen counter,
always two giant pots of two kinds'a soup
    hot on the stove,
you slowly look over it all & choose this, choose that…
                And quietly are people talking here,
& in the living room, noticeably are voices
    kept soft & quiet,
an ambient soft music plays, soft light of lamps,
an atmosphere of hushed tranquility pervades,
it is a sanctuary of peacefulness here,
in this exquisitely arranged & perfectly, consciously,
precisely maintained, living space…
                            Everything is placed
in an interconnected feng shui balanced wholeness—
Any little change, any new, acquired item to display,
    Peggy says,
reverberates throughout the room till everything
once again finds its proper, energetic placement.
Every year, she says, she rearranges the whole
according to the new energies of the year.

You see these standing geodes at & near the front door,
a little desk light highlighting one…a bowl of egg rocks,
    a standup shelf of books,
                      & there's a winding staircase
in an outside enclosed potted plant glass column
up to the 2nd floor bedroom space…
                    There're little assemblies
of rocks & crystals—smoothly rounded spheres
of all kinds you see—tuning forks set out & a big, crystal
singing bowl on a counter,
                & little Quan Yin altars
& Buddhas, paintings on all the walls,
a fireplace insert warm & constant, cushy sofa & chairs
    —a cat is asleep atop one of the chairs—,
more books lined along on a low shelf, in front of which
a display box of business cards, card decks, booklets,
    all neatly arranged…
                & books about labyrinths
—a hint—sit on a coffee table, get scattered about
—last year a copy of my *Through The Labyrinth,*
A guided astrological meditation I saw—
Everything in the room looks exactly, precisely,
perfectly placed…each individual item
    in its place.
               And so what about Peggy?

    Think *SOUND.*
Peggy works with sound, the energetics of sound,
a long-time healer, she discovered the potencies of vibration.
She conducts meditative, exploratory, voice channeling
    gatherings…
her house is a nexus for all kinds'a healers.

        Out the windows
a pleasant meadow rolls away
looking back towards town…
you can see to a far ridge of the Santa Cruz Mountains,
& Sun is lighting up the near Felton ridge…

                                      But—then—
What so many come for, the traditional personal ritual
    —oh, the hint already was noted—
is out the back door—
                    Beyond the triple-level fountain,
reeds & bamboo, altars, bowls, crystals, big round rocks,
the Quan Yins, prayer flags, the tables
    & circle of chairs…is
               the Labyrinth—
a smallish, circular labyrinth designed of stones,
laid out on some all-weather fabric material,
    a large rock sits in the center…
& dozens & dozens of people, at their own individual
    timing,
            walk this Labyrinth,
throughout the day, they come & go…
The invitation is there—
        Pause a moment first—
        When you are ready,
        enter—

Start the New Year walking the Labyrinth,
a time for personal musing & worldly reflection,
a time for New Years wishes…

                And Summer,
in a purple cape & Happy New Year crown,
is this moment alone in the Labyrinth,
she is walking ever so slowly…& pausing…
spreading her cape at moments,
she is in a zone of her own,
        she is going round, going round…
A long time she circles & circles
the center point rock…

             And time too
to write down messages of hope
    for the New Year

on strips of paper sitting on a table
at the circle of chairs,
& then hanging them
from branches of a tree…

        And you see
words posted about
that Peggy attunes to—
There is one in particular
you might have noticed—
She seems especially
to like the word

        JOY

Felton
January 1, 2017

Pacific Ave Halloween

This is the night when they all come out—
This is the night when you just might lose yourself.
This is the really crazy night, this is the madness all come out night.
This is the night of streams from the strange & weird hinterlands converging
    upon our town.
This is the parade of ocean washed ashore phantasmagoria on Pacific Ave,
this night of the crushing waves & waves of the promenade, back & forth,
    & back & forth,
        how they sweep & how they sweep the full-length overflowing
            both sides the Ave—
This is the night of anything you might imagine, whatever is whatever this night—
This night of the grotesque, the ridiculous, the fabulous & outrageous.
This night of harlequins, of the bizarre & creepy, of clowns & the absolutely goofy.
This night of risqué, of unexpected temptations, of free-floating roving desires.
This night of big hair & all the queen's makeup, of the trans-dressed & androgynous.
This night of creatures, monsters, elves & fairies, ghosts, ghouls, gremlins & gnomes,
    of werewolves, warlocks & witches.
This night of butterflies, angels & space aliens, of future cyborgs, androids & robots.
This is the night of the thronging throngs of the unconscious gushing forth,
    of subpersonalities let loose by the thousands—
        20,000 converged on the Ave, they say of this night.
This night of the Face—faces, faces, the compulsive looking into faces,
masked or unmasked, partially hidden, utterly Other, whatever, it doesn't matter,
    it's the compulsive looking into faces looking back,
looking into faces of who or what we are below the surface revealing—
    Faces of another of who we might be.
Endless the posing of our madness, the pictures taken, the so willing exhibitionists
    & everyone a voyeur.
This is the night you wonder just who all these people are.
This is the night your own secret interior goes flaunting out in the public
    without a blush.

This year the city brings out the floodlights like an eerie, lunar-light-bathed day—
You swim through it all, & you hear the beat, the beat, you hear the intensities
    of beat & rhythm going out all around you,
the surfeit of overwhelm, of a swimming in too much, of all senses overload.
And the voices, the voices, the roar of voices, like all the faces, faces, faces,
    a vortex swirling
               in the sea,
            a VORTEX—

But you hear no screams here—the screams are elsewhere.

November 2005

That She inspires

That She inspires this place/rules this place—
No mere coincidence this is a feminist town,
why all orientations/progressive persuasions
    find sanctuary here.
She is the ultimate, opened-armed, omni-expression,
freely-giving Fountain of Divinity—

        If you look out over Monterey Bay
        & utterly open yourself to Her,
        you will witness the Vision of Her—
        She rises resplendent & mercurial
        out of the Fountain of the Bay,
        & She opens her arms & says,
            Come, here is your haven,
            you who suffer intolerance,
            you who have never known acceptance—
            You, the oddball, eccentric, out there,
            you who were somehow attuned differently,
            into my arms you are welcome.

early 1990s

Pride Day

Paradin' down Pacific Ave
it's the Lesbian, Gay, Bisexual, Transgender Pride
    Santa Cruz 25th Year Anniversary Parade
& I'm walkin' this a first year ever in the transgender contingent—
Kind'a overcast so far, surprisin' not too many people,
maybe it's the weather, maybe 'cause parade's earlier this year,
    but we're all like paradin' proud the Ave,
& there's a turn right at Water St., cops clearin' the way, car's honkin',
& Joy is just dancin' merrily along, wavin' round the trans banner,
someone's on bongo,
                & over the bridge to San Lorenzo Park
the whole shebang settles into all the prideful booths
under the June Sunday Sun finally comin' out,
    suddenly it's gettin' kind'a hot—
There's a big stage of speakers, music, singers, comic from SF,
people swarmin' all over, everyone circulatin', meetin' old friends,
    meetin' new friends,
                just meetin' whomever,
& photos are taken of us transgendered sittin' at this no shade table
    gettin' a little sunburned now,
while this cheery gal is passin' out flavored, candy-color lubricants.

It's the great diversity celebration of the multi-poly-many-expression,
whatever orientation this big wide flarin' human family is—
There're all sorts'a styles, & all are, like, lettin' it all out—
Dykes on bikes, guys in drag, nuns lookin' proper, the bare breasted
& bare asses stickin' out skimpy affairs, lots of skin, leather, tatooes,
piercings, rings, feathers, costumes, makeup, or au naturale...
                from grungy to dressy,

it's the rich multi-diverse universe
    of humans
              unstopped, uncaged, uninhibited,
it's like the liberated pride of all we are
here to celebrate what all the Sun puts forth—

              And here's trans Trin
finally put on her dress & orange wig
& is, like, into posin' pleasurably for pictures…

June 2000

Wharf to Wharf

They couldn't have asked for a better mornin'
is what the announcer said—
        Seems the best day for the race
in 15 years,
that is, if the heat doesn't prove to be too much,
for it's clear risin' Sun; high above, wisps of cloud;
warmin' up already at 8 am—
                You have'ta look far off
      to the West
   & you see a purplish bank of chilling fog;
but out across the Bay
        it's so remarkably calm, like a mirror,
          you cannot see a wave,
       not one wave.

It's the 28th Annual Wharf to Wharf Race
startin' here in The Cruz down on Beach Street,
front of Cocoanut Grove, next the Municipal Wharf,
            goin' 6 miles out to Capitola village,
finishing at the wharf there,
14,000 official runners & probably more besides
literally pack every square inch of this long beach-fronted block.

        And a gal is singin' the Star Spangled Banner,
'bout 3 Beach Boys classics come up next,
      & it's nearing—just about—8:30
& the announcer who's been doin' this thing
   for all these 28 years
        says *Get ready*
     & suddenly, this, like, cannon goes off
& on this gorgeous, placid, fog-free, so perfect of a summery morning
   the race begins.

         I find myself standin' at the starting line
watchin' wave after wave—they're all ages—of hundreds
   of runners go by,
& after 5 minutes hundreds

                    are still crossin' the line
            as the forefront runners,
      —the announcer informs—
have already advanced over a mile out.
                    And it's 8 minutes into the race
& the last of the runners are only now reaching
      the start of it;
at almost 10 minutes a few stragglers are still just startin',
while barely 18 minutes later the winner will already be crossin'
      the Capitola finish line.

                  And along the way,
they all get entertained & pepped up
      by these impromptu fun bands playin' out
                      on driveways & sidewalks,
& the runners get sprayed down with hoses, if they want,
      for the heat;
there's a pit stop at the Yacht Harbor for water
      for those in need—
The forefront runners, of course, are in it to compete,
but all the rest are goin' at their own pace of endurance,
simply enjoying it for the thrill of it,
      & the intensity of it,
for the participation & official recognition
      that they
            have done it.

                  And now,
almost two hours later,
the last runners are nearin' the village
      of little Capitola-by-the-Sea,
where—it figures—
            there's quite a fog come in,
      suddenly chill enough
for spectators
            to put on jackets
      & zip up.

July 2000

Beach Boardwalk July 4th

                            About one-thirty
the Sun broke through, though the fog
—often a spoiler of early summer—made only a short retreat,
    a mile or so out.
                        I walk down the slope
from Santa Cruz West Coast Hotel (the old Dream Inn)
& most beautiful appear the tall palms that line the sidewalk
    of Beach Street.
High flying, of course, the Stars & Stripes, high upon a pole
    atop Cocoanut Grove.

                      And there are people,
of course. So many people, streams of people—
Where do they all come from? Oh, they come from everywhere.
    We know Earth is bountiful.
Every year they come. Every day summertime they come.
Today just happens to be July 4th.
                            And they converge
upon this Santa Cruz image-making machine sending out
its visions of American amusement, its siren call sounding,
Come! Come & have fun! It's the Santa Cruz Beach Boardwalk!
And it's, like, the only boardwalk you'll find along the whole long
    West Coast—

                               And the beach here
is heavily peppered with people, sitting & lying on blankets,
standing & staring & just cruisin' the crowd, enjoying picnic lunches,
volley ball jumping where nets are set up, a few daring the cold
of Bay water, most happy for the Sun, warm, not quite hot,
though bathing suits & shorts, bare feet & chests, are plenty.
    Plenty of bodies out on the beach
& a few elegant, white sailboats & sleek, white cabin cruisers
    picturesque on the Bay, this side the fog;
& the Santa Cruz Municipal Wharf, to the right, is lined with cars

    & continuous streams of on-foot visitors.
Everywhere, plenty of people, plenty of bodies,
    plenty of Fourth of July fun.
            This *is* the American holiday, after all.
There are American boys & American girls,
American teens & couples & families of all sizes,
    American groups of all kinds;
& there're singles boppin' along, checkin' things out;
you sense a gang presence too, but security & police are always visible—
American crowds—& plenty of foreigners, too—all converged
    on the quintessential Cruz.
Oddly, perhaps, a man in East Indian dress—emerald green tunic
over white, head wrapped in a turban in white; long, two-pronged,
    wavy beard; bare foot;
            his ten-speed bike loaded down with packs,
an American flag hoisted from a rack on a makeshift pole,
    reads to all who will listen
        from his miniature Bible.
                And a white-bearded man
with head band & shades has a knack with fingers
for turning pampas grass leaves into little rose flowers
he offers to people who gladly line up for them,
    his little American flag
        propped in a green painted can.
                Another man nearby,
dressed in red & white, twists sausage long balloons
    into different kinds of head gear,
a young girl sitting on a bicycle hangs out with him wearing one,
    an ET Grey face bobbing above.
                And another man
with guitar, pulled back ponytail, his American flag
propped up in a guitar case, sings,
    I watch the ocean change color...
    I am but a piece of driftwood...

                              And I walk on this day—
I walk on & immediately I enter the big Casino Fun Center,
an exploding arcade bonanza of games just inside the doors
       of Cocoanut Grove,
                              & the blast of it slams me,
this suddenly darkened, cavernous, moody blue interior
       the moment you first walk in,
              or call it a madhouse of sight & sound—
It slams you—the rows of dim track lighting on grid work above,
       strings of game lights flashing & lights pulsing;
a pervasive, low, background rumble, with bells, bonks, blasts, whiz bangs,
& more ring rings & rat-a-tat-tats & whams & whistles & pinball boinks
& whacks & groans & thuds from video game battles & vehicles of one kind
or another crash & burn, & more ring rings & air hockey disks are loud
smacked around tables & balls are rolling & shots are fired,
       you can hardly hear voices above it all.
And voices there are. Packed with people. Especially young people
       playin' 'em all—
                       Dozens & dozens of games
sardine-packed by the aisle in this fun mad central:
Pinball Star Wars/Stargate/Star Trek/Comet/Whirlwind/Twister/
Hurricane/Cyclone/Superman/Radical/Street Fighter/Jurassic Park/
High Speed/Phantom of the Opera/Genie/even Dolly Parton—
And there're video games of high-violence Primal Rage/Mortal Kombat/
Martial Champion/Virtua Fighter/Marvel Super Heroes/fighter jet
Raiden Fighters/Terminator/X-Men/vicious kung fu fighting Tekken/
& there's football Blitz/NBA Jam/The Lost World/Asteroids/
       & enter a stand-up booth for Discs Tron.
                              And a kid speeds too fast
in his attempt to outwit a snaky California highway,
       trying to match California Speed,
              all these distractions, obstacles in a blink,
                     & I get dizzy just watchin';
same with Alpine Racer/Wave Runner/Top Skater/Surf Planet/
       Daytona USA 1, 2, 3 & 4, & so many more—
All are pumped up on speed, reflex, action, sound, bursts of sound,
       instant sound, impact sound, *loud* sound—
Or jump on a motorcycle, soar through canyons on a Prop Cycle,

or take a race car driver seat or a jet fighter pilot cockpit seat;
& a teen shoots a hand held gun & blows away opponents
down brick solid dungeon corridors & outside these Gothic castle
    parked limos
               in the game of Time Crisis;
& people wait outside a darkened room for Laser Tag—
A sign flashes, *The ultimate in interactive.*

And in the real world of real foes, real crises,
might we ask,
              Who among us are the real heroes?

                        And there's
an Old West-style Gold Rush Shooting Gallery,
& dress up for Old Time Portrait Studio, & have a fortune read
in cards by dame mannequins behind glass, & stuffed animals
    are piled & packed & peek out from behind glass;
get morphed in a Foto Morphosis booth, or put on tomorrow's
Virtual Reality helmets like some high-tech pilot as video monitors
    follow the action.

                    And I move through it all,
moving on through this world, in my brief passage
    through this world—
I exit to the Boardwalk into some light again, & start down
    the long, partially enclosed of a walkway;
streaming the center ceiling a triple row of pulsing running lights
    lead you on,
               O I am caught in the drift of it all,
                    there's so much more still hits you—
To the left, all the candy & gift & Sun & surf shops; to the right,
    the arched vistas upon beach & Bay.
And next the Cannonball Arcade is Neptune's Kingdom
    I now slip into—
I pass a food joint & Fantasy Image (Your Face—Anyplace)
    & then this Ask the Brain smarty face—

An eerily lifelike, bald-pate, monocle-eyed, electrostatic discharging,
smug-smiling mad doctor behind glass,
                      & I see I am suddenly inside Neptune's Kingdom
of a giant arched ceiling room with a miniature golf pirate theme.
On the far high wall a sailing ship replica marooned on rocks
protrudes out a big painting depicting some imagined ideal
     of a tropical cove—
There's a volcano spouting smoke & lighted sparks;
    & then I see more games packed in right behind me—
A Smuggler's Arcade, with take the wheel & high speed
     through San Francisco,
         or get inside a Rad Mobile;
            jump in a seat & take controls of Cyber Sled;
& there is more—
Dungeons & Dragons/Aero Fighters/Rampage/Terminator 2
Judgement Day/Steel Gunner/giant console, wide-screen X-Men
& big life screen Old West Mad Dog, & take a gun, step forward,
    & start to shoot in Time Crisis II;
& inside the hologram Time Traveler a miniature, blue-clad woman
in these big, blue boots materializes out of a bubble,
    Greetings, I am Kyla, Princess of the Galactic Federation.
    I journey through time to find you.
    We need your help... You are our last hope...

And in the real world of real time travel, real Galactic Federations,
might we ask,
         Who among us holds the real key to futurity?

                      And upstairs
there're more games, air hockey tables, pool tables,
a draft beer bar is there & historical photos line the wall,
& people are pouring over & milling about,
    streaming the stairs up & down.

                     And I walk out
& walk on into bright sunlight again in the open air
& the crowds of Independence Day promenade in waves
    that irresistibly sweep along,

descending steps to the beach, exiting the beach,
going to & fro among arcades & concession stands & rooms
of Pokereno/Boom Ball & Skee Ball & all the typical booths you find
    of stuffed animal games;
there're people wandering alone or as couples, people in groups,
parents
    with kids,
some sitting, eating at tables & benches, chatting with each other,
or waiting in lines for thrills & screams & heartbeat workouts,
    all intent on having fun,
        indulging all the while on their American candy apples/
popcorn/hotdogs & corndogs/pretzels/tacos/burgers & fries/
cotton candy/sno cones/ice cream/sundaes/milk shakes/
    American soda pop & American beer.

              And they ride
the amusement visions of America—
Pirate Ship/Speed Bumps bumper cars/Haunted Castle/
Giant Dipper screaming people historic rollercoaster/Wave Jammer/
stomach-turning Chaos & Typhoon/Bermuda Triangle/Rip Tide/
Rock-o-Plane/Venturer like Jonah swallowed in a high-tech whale;
& still, there're more rides, at the far end, a quarter mile down—
Video Storm & Ferris Wheel & the splashy wet log coaster
    of Logger's Revenge,
        & a whole lower level you surprisingly discover there
    packed with more still.
               And a cable trolley Sky Glider
shuttles people back & forth overhead
    —get how the bird's eye sees it all—;
& the constant scream of voices letting loose utterly fills the air;
    & wafting surf tunes of Beach Boys you hear
        throughout the air
               in this time warp of a capsule
    of pop culture Americana.
Out on the beach a giant stage is set up
    where Friday night guest bands from the past
      will play
          for Summertime Summer Nights.

                              And in a room all its own
—you can't miss it—, you find the childhood charm
    we have all certainly known
                    of Merry-Go-Round.
You can see how people love it, how they line up & jump on,
& round & round, up & down, how the mock horses prance;
& the tinkly, mesmeric, carousel music, it goes round & round;
& lights above radiating on spokes out from the center are turning,
    round & round;
& mirrors flash on the perimeter of the rotating ring,
there're all these mirrors on the walls,
    everything is bright & reflective & glittery—

And in the real world of real Visions, real action,
might we ask,
            Who among us are the real prophets?
            Who are the world's real movers & shakers?

    Here,
the American-born visions of amusement bring in the people—
And so many people, streams of people. Where do they all
    come from?
Oh, they come from everywhere. We know Earth is bountiful.
And Earth will be bountiful, no matter what
                            the Ocean
                might bring—

        A mile out in the Bay,
a solid bank of spoiler fog,
looking in all the world like an impending wall of water.

Santa Cruz
July 1998

A Summertime Summer Night

This is the kind'a night everyone has'ta love,
    such a night like this,
                    to remember—
                                It's balmy, early August,
sky is utterly clear, a deep deep blue that turns
    to a stilled liquid black,
but for the brightness of a gibbous Moon,
its scintillating of silvery light a splayed necklace
    out upon the Bay;
& to deeply breathe in the briny tonic aroma of the air,
to see the cool hues of muted lights strung all along the length
    of the wharf,
their reflections on the calm, dark body of hushed water
    below—
           OH!

                    This is Friday night,
weekly free concert night of summertime here
packing our famous, always-ever-so-popular
Santa Cruz Beach Boardwalk—
           So many, so many people here—
Flowing & flowing the currents of people here,
& all the shouts & screams of kids in a nonstop whirl,
screams that come in waves as cars of the roller coasters
    suddenly plummet in a heart-stop;
                all the adrenaline rush of intensity
    of a cacophonous riot of sound
                      you hear from end to end
of this amusement land to escape into, packed with arcades,
packed with games & rides & food stands,
packed with people, all the young getting in their fill of thrills,
it's as classic of a Boardwalk as you would find anywhere
    in the world.
                A kaleidoscope of pulsing & flashing lights,
the strobe-like flash of lights of the big round of Ferris wheel,
the fast moving running lights of the landmark Giant Dipper
& crisscrossing pendulum swinging lights of Typhoon—

Everywhere the glamour of lights, the bright shout of lights,
    lights & lights & lights
                to dazzle & excite—

People pack the sands out from the spotlight all lit up
    big, 7-foot raised stage
                out on the beach,
& all these kids are playin' out from the fringes
    of the crowd—
Packed the main level walk-through of Boardwalk
    just opposite the stage,
packed the steps & sloped walkway to the second level
    facing the stage,
                packed the second level there—
All packed to hear tonight
        out of the past
                Davy Jones
    of the former Sixties group
        The Monkees
                sing
            & bring back memories—
Pink & lime green the backdrop stage lights,
long banks of spots shinin' down from the big metal framework
    built high up above the stage,
          & the Sky Glider with its little, two-person scoops
    shuttles people back & forth in mid-air,
                    passing directly overhead
    those of us watchin' from the steps.

              Such a night is this—
And Davy Jones obliges the crowd,
as he & current backup band play a number
    of the old Sixties hits,
            among others,
& so many, so many in this crowd who lived at that time
—oh, you can see how many of them there are,
        the older adults of this crowd—
remember those songs, remember those days,
    remember those special years—

A cascade of flashback memories
    goes back to that time;
                it is a tear that comes
to remember how extraordinary that time,
for so many here like no other since,
    that time we knew
               as the Sixties—

    But then I saw her face...
    now I'm a believer...

Yes, I saw Her face out here
    this night—
One face of all Her faces,
Our Goddess, The Cruz.

Santa Cruz Beach Boardwalk
(August 2003)/September 2004

Romantic at Capitola Beach

    When full Moon comes rising
over the eastward Bay
& the Esplanade's nightclubs & restaurants fill
  with clamorous people
amidst the blast of dance music on a hot Friday night,
but your desire is to get just beyond it, down the sidewalk,
along the beach, where the benches are quiet with quiet-talking
  couples & close friends;
or, if you wish, go further, there, where the terrace
of a walkway of seawall is sheer-edged to the restless rocking
  of wave below,
      & the broad Moon lit water shines like silver
& you see the coastal lights sparkling round the curve of Bay
—Seacliff, Rio Del Mar, Seascape, La Selva, Pajaro Dunes—,
but south Seaside & Monterey & Pacific Grove you cannot see
  for summer fog;
& the strung lit pearls that wrap round Zelda's outside seating
  look so inviting;
& further still, to the right, not far beyond, Capitola wharf you see,
its lamps of amber softness warm glowing in equanimity
  along its length,
      restaurant lights culminating,
& you see silhouettes of fishing boats cross the lunar way;
as you gather it all & all is here, in one sweep, compact & still,
& there is only the sonance of surf, cadenced & sweet
—such a ravishing evening in little Capitola-by-the-Sea—,
who would not take an opportunity such as this
  to sit quietly with a date or lover,
   & share with each other all that the heart whispers,
& perhaps touch & kiss as she & I did years ago,
with tall eucalyptus crowning the rising of cliff above you
& rhythm of rock tide & backwash gently lapping
  & sloshing below,
with an occasional wake-up wave that hits hard,
to come splashing over the railing of seawall—
To sit quietly & kiss on a night like this,
  what could be more exquisite?

                              And King Jupiter
now ascends the throne of coastal lights
regal in the numinosity of Moon's fullness.
And comes right up the Light of the Goddess Herself
& does a scintillating dance on silver dazzling feet.

Capitola-by-the-Sea
August 1998

An Afternoon in Felton

A Sunday summer afternoon
& right smack in the middle of the old historic
    Felton Covered Bridge
                      a group is gathered—
They say they get together every Sunday afternoon
    to do this gig—
That is, the gig they do is to set goin' a beat;
it's some serious drummin' they're doin'—
They got a pair of Brazilian congas,
a sheika & djembe from Africa, a dunbek from Turkey,
Mexican claves, a cowbell from good ole America,
    & whatever else—
Oh yeah, one guy's blowin' a didgeridoo,
    from Out Back Australia.
They're goin' at it, alright, kind'a pullin' in
& capturin' as audience whoever's passin' through.

                      And through one
of the big, wood-beamed, rectangular windows
    I happen look out of,
        I see the shallow San Lorenzo River
    lazily flowing below;
it's sand bar exposed one spot, hit dry by the Sun;
& a big willow's droopin' inside the view;
I look up & twistin' wisps of cirrus are silent on high—
It's a different kind'a music happenin' up there—
But, for us, here, there's a powerful Earth beat
    keeps a-goin'.
                It's a Sunday afternoon…

(August 2000)
December 2000

Full Moon in June

      It's like,
you must've heard somewhere—
There's a full Moon in June
    & it's,
       on top of that,
 a full Moon *Cruz*,
      & even,
    another notch more—
      it's Friday the 13th,
 & it's all
kind'a makin' the Pacific Avenue scene
  happenin'
     this evening—
    Like, it's boppin' along time,
      cruz'n The Cruz time,
    it's hangin' out
       & checkin' everyone out time,
  it's the dude's are dude'n it time,
    it's the Kuzanga 7-piece marimba beat time—
Yep, they're all set up
      'cross from
    big Cinema 9,
   a crowd they got,
    like, they're all congregatin'.
It's the dance time
     of gettin' in the groove,
       the rain of mallets
    strikin' & strikin' those bars,
   it's the beat makin' of rhythm time—
It's like,
   "a vision of a cheeseburger" time
      the man's sign said,
   a little box he set out
     for handout money,

                or it's
                        Any spare change?
                                another walked along & asked,
                    said he would give me some tequila,
                                    but I didn't want that—
        or like,
                    it's visions of girls, girls
                                        everywhere
                        up & down Pacific Ave,
    it's like,
                here we all are,
                        all playin' at bein' human,
            whatever our role might be—

                Whatever,
            it's like,
                    to-go coffee & cappuccino,
                            mochas perhaps,
                                Santa Cruz Coffee Roasting time—
        It's the wake up of desire time,
                        the honey-colored full Moon
                                    rising time,
    it's like,
            eatin' honey spread all over
                                honey-Moon of June—
                She knew such lore
                            & shared it freely,
                    between her sets,
                        we happened to speak briefly—
    It's like,
                an electrical current runnin' thru
                    all sentient beings of Earth this night
            of a honey-Moon full Moon,
                                the mad Moon
                        like a crazy tune—
                It's like,
                        all the guitars they're strummin',
            the thumpin' & beatin' on whatever kind'a
                            makeshift drums,

                it's the portable organ,
                        she's sittin' on the bench,
                                it's in her lap,
                                        it's the tune she's playin',
                gatherin' all the
                                        sidewalk nomads,
                blankets & backpacks
                                & all kinds'a stuff laid out,
                street life a'livin',
                                & still,
                                people keep'a cruz'n—

                                        It's like,
all the eatin' & drinkin' establishments
        everyone's flockin' to,
                all the
                                jivin' goin' on,
                all the
                                deals
                apparently goin' down,
        which is funny
                        why
                        with my notepad & pen
        couple dudes thought
                                I might have been
                a cop undercover
        —with my hair long so,
                        my androgynous no denyin' look,
                                come on, dudes—
                but there's one that knew better
                                & said,
                        I was a poet—

It's like,
                the waft of pizza
                        over the tables outside
                                        Pizza My Heart,
        it's the cookies of Pacific Cookie
                makin' their way on the street,

it's the ice cream of Marini
       they're lickin',
    sittin' over there,
it's the all new Del Mar neon marquee
        pulsin' manic
   like a heart on speed—
It's the imbibe of Moonshine,
     the makin' loony
    tune time—

     And out of thee blue
  this guy called out,
       Write us a song
 & so I said,
     I'd do what I can
      & weave that in,
  but it wasn't until
     I caught that glimpse
   of the honeyed Moon—
It's like,
    suddenly that moment
     She offered me
   Her drink
  & of it
    I drank,
& it sure hit me fast—

Somewhere you've heard
   there's a full Moon in June,
    it's a crazy sort'a tune,
 & I almost missed it.

June 13, 2003

The Seers Circle

A circle we gathered Saturday evening in the Big Dome,
    a Seers Circle we gathered,
and so intention of our purpose to the universe we sent out in thought—
Guiding spirits that surround us, that might they hear us, were invoked;
come, help us to understand such changes that were now abounding
    in our world.
And so questions individuals posed about events & issues of the day,
and those called to be the Voice of a Seer spoke out in reply.
Hushed, attentive, how we all sat there, listening, listening,
    as the seers revealed to us what they could see,
              what they were able by tongue to tell.
Out of the silence it was amazing such things we heard.

Last to speak was Kelley, who I knew—
And she spoke about the Heart, about the powerful, enormous
    reality of the Heart.
And from the Heart, we all said a prayer, & then names
were spoken aloud by those who were so moved,
    for loved ones in need of prayer,
              and spontaneously,
through some metamorphosis of the moment,
sudden impressions of the outside world, Nature Herself,
came out of the silence receptive to our kinship prayers,
so that person after person—whoever, again, was so moved—
now named the stream, the butterfly, the joy of sunlight,
the flower & meadow, the Moon, the hummingbird & redwood,
the play & laughter of children, soar of the hawk,
    the vast oceans,
        I said.
        And then hands we held,
person linked with person,

    in the great round of this festival family
        in the fading light of dusk
            outside the dome windows,
as music of flamenco guitar entertained us now,
a singer a song we heard & then another,
a belly dancer came forward & delighted us all,
and three women, a tight circle sitting on the floor,
caressed each other to the music amidst the clapping,
the fractal play of a light show on the curve of dome above,
the energy of all—you could feel it—rising & rising,
    peaking to
        a wonderful,
            sweeping through us all

                EPIPHANY

Outside, the still fading light of dusk...

August 5, 2006
Satir Satori Salon Samurai Sundance Consciousness-Raising Festival
Virginia Satir Conceptual Art Center, Ben Lomond

Upon leaving the bookstore

Glad to step out into the pink of the young evening,
glad to see others engaging the promise so apparent
of the suggestive smile of the evening—
                                    Glad to speak with you,
it means so much that words still need the living breath
    of lungs—
Oh, the most luscious and sweet among them
    are born straight from the tongue—
The evening hints of kisses & even more.
I should like to write in a book what words are for,
how they sing in the wild Moon glass of this wine pink
    evening—
Perhaps someone will step outside some years from now,
inspired by a word glanced upon, glad & glad & glad,
and utter some such words as mine
    that spring
                straight from the tongue.

August 2003
Logos Used Books
Pacific Ave

Synergy Party

brainchild of
Paul Gaylon & Joey Shepp

Like, what's up?
You say
there's another new thing happenin'
in The Cruz?

Well, you gotta tune in, check out
the new networking of something hot *is* happening here
with Synergy Party—
Started in 2002,
a whatever occasional, sometimes monthly affair,
perhaps—who knows—they'll get to be
quite regular, even—
Consider them
your kind'a party,
what you yourself might think to do
to foster an informed community,
bringing a diversity of persons & groups, all sorts of
progressive, socially conscious & activist organizations,
cutting-edge environmentally friendly businesses
together
to be able to
present who they are,
with their
movin' along mini-presentations,
it's
an all manner of sharing & introducing ourselves
& networking opportunity,
plus music & performance art & celebrating one another
sort'a gig,

                    it's
        a way of makin' community
                            so that we
            become aware
                of what's at play,
        so that we might become
            involved ourselves
                        & make somethin' that's evolvin',
                all of us
                        workin' together,
            in one way or another,
in advancing the great cause
        of people
                doin' good
                            for the planet—
Like, it's the synergy of it all—*get it?*
    That parts/persons
comin' together in creating community,
            in a synthesis of how all is interacting,
is greater, something more, something perhaps novel,
        something perhaps unexpected,
            with new possibilities inspired,
than isolated parts or persons
                        could make happen
                on their own—

It's the new happenin' thing,
& was birthed
            right here,
    in the Vortex

        of *The Cruz*.

June 2003

Driving Highway 17

It happens to be the main artery into & out of The Cruz,
    direction north, from the Valley,
this roller coaster of a drive called Highway 17,
snaking through the dark, tranquility-loving redwood,
oak & pine & laurel & madrone dense Santa Cruz Mountains;
barely 20 miles the transit across these mountains—
They say tens of thousands pass over the Summit every day;
every Monday through Friday, early morning, late afternoon,
a continuous, fast-moving caravan of commuters goes forth
    & returns
—it's the daily, no-choice-in-the-matter nightmare of so many—
from The Cruz sittin' pretty on the Bay
—comin' back, if you're lucky, you'll catch glimpses
    of the Goddess, at certain points—
        the curvature of Her pale blue body,
    cleavage of mountain,
    Her sparkling necklace at night you'll see,
    if it's clear,
        over 40 miles distant is Monterey—
from The Cruz they stream into the Valley,
    where the jobs are
        —Silicon Valley, of course—.

    I'm drivin' the hill,
      as they say,
    goin' over the Summit—

But it's also a killer, this highway,
must be one of the most dangerous stretches of high traffic flow
    in the country,
a stream pushin' to 60 mph round curves meant for 40-45 or so;
& of course, if you're drivin' it regular like, you certainly know about
    the accidents—
        Oh, you certainly have seen your share of 'em,
      & chain reactions of 'em,
& vehicles backed up for winding miles, & you're helplessly
    caught up in it;

in the rainy season, count on them just about every day—
Some days, says a friend, *I pass 1-2-3 happenin'*
before my eyes & wonder how I've managed to escape once again.

You never know what to expect on this highway—
You see cars flipped over, crumpled up, vans ripped open,
burned out shells of vehicles, big rigs jackknifed & spilled out
their load—
    it's all over the road—
       Definitely a treacherous ride if you push it—
Hot shot gotta get somewhere over the Summit fast guys push it,
  their luck—
& sure enough you'll see one of 'em wind up rolled over
  or flyin' down an embankment…
Or consider goin' round a blind curve at night doin' 45
& a car's dead stop stalled a second ahead in your lane—
Just hope you can swerve, the other lane is free…

A sign does warn you:
After a few easy miles of slow rise prelude
passing the bushy-blooming skirt of sedate Scotts Valley,
you see it flashing:

> *Winding Road*
> *next 8 miles*
> *Drive Carefully*

And the curves get sharper, cut through the sides
of offended mountain; and rock slides get common,
if it's serious rain; there's always bound to be some kind'a mess
  along the side
      to clean up—
And the view out there, taking each curve, gets better & better,
but better keep your eye
      on the road—
         And nearin' the Summit
there's a straightaway stretch—they got food stops
on both sides—, with the backbone ridge of blunt-topped Loma Prieta
  on the right, imposing looking,

the distant ridge of closer-to-the-coast mountain on the left,
    westward, sunset looking;
it's a somewhat safer zone this short, straightaway stretch
before again the curves to the marker of the Summit—
And here it is already,
                   Patchen Pass, 1800 feet elevation—
But everyone knows it simply as *The Summit*.

                 And there's somethin'
always eerie about this point of the Summit,
how it has this atmosphere of otherness about it—
remote, closed in by the dark, held-at-bay forest,
'specially at night, the feeling of,
    there's something different here,
& the feeling's gone as you round the next bend
& so quickly now you're goin' down the other side,
rounding the curves of increasing centrifugal motion—
Careful, careful, of those curves, how fast you're goin'.

              And shortly you're passin' Lexington Reservoir
—its level seasonally & wildly variable—
approachin' the gateway of the Valley,
    the gem of Los Gatos—
If the day's relatively clear, you will see momentarily
the drier, scrubbier, desert-like looking Diablo Range mountains
    beyond distant San Jose;
you can always gauge from here what the smog
    is like there—
If all you see is the dirty haze,
you know you're going to be entering some bad air.

                In the summer, on weekends,
they'll be floodin' in from the Valley,
they all wanna hit the Santa Cruz Beach Boardwalk & the sands
    of The Cruz;
it'll be bumper to bumper for miles the better the weather;
nearin' sunset it'll be the exact same caravan sluggishly
    making its way back—
Only hope no accident makes the trip even longer.

You wonder if someday somethin' might be done
    to end the nightmare,
like some mass transit system of a solution,

                  over The Summit,
        as they say—

What will it take?
Well, without somethin' done,
you know it will only get worse—
Do I need to say it again?
Without somethin' done,
    every year,
it can only get worse!

April 2001

The Acacias

You can't miss 'em,
    'cause they're bloomin' all over—
You can always tell it's somethin' like spring,
           here, already,
      even if it's
          January,
   & winter rains
        —& perhaps we'll still even see
         —*it is* a possibility—
         a little flurry of snow—,
the rains of winter, yes,
   still have all the months
      of Feb & March to go,
  but,
      that's the way it is along the coast,
        this springing of the year
     spread out over months,
         blazin' in stages—
  Yes,
it's somethin' like spring
with the acacias bloomin'—
You can't miss 'em,
     'cause they're all along the freeway
        —Highway 1 from the south,
  or especially if you're headin' north up 17
       towards Scotts Valley way—
You can't miss 'em,
    'cause they're blazin' blazin' YELLOW
      all over.

January 2002

Bonny Doon

Bonny Doon?
What a name is that?
So where is this Bonny Doon?
We have all heard the question.
It is one of the best-kept secrets of the county.
Bonny Doon is certainly a mysterious place.
It is not always found on a map.
It is not a town, not even a hamlet,
has no central point, not even a single store,
but we can only say it is a special place,
a mysterious place, up on the plateau
     of Ben Lomond Mountain—
From windy Felton Empire Rd.
going up from Felton, or even windier,
steeper, Alba Rd. going up from Ben Lomond,
where both roads end at Empire Grade,
running miles along the heavily wooded ridge
—but what views suddenly appear of other
far distant Santa Cruz Mountain ridges!—
Bonny Doon is an unseen, hidden, secret place…
All you see at first are the trees…& trees.
Or, it is reached by Empire Grade beginning
miles away, to the south, at UCSC.
               On the far, western side,
it eventually slopes down via Bonny Doon Rd.
to the Pacific Ocean, near Davenport,
     to the north.
Yes, hidden among the trees, with its snaky roads,
it lays out with flattened stretches in places
     like Martin Rd.
that get blazing hot in the open summer Sun.
Wildfires—four of them, we hear, since 1948—
have blazed through here over the years—
And how many homes tragically burned
just this summer in the most devastating
of fires in the Santa Cruz Mountains.

Despite the devil of fire, Bonny Dooners
remain committed to what they call
this slice of heaven.

                        Try to even guess
how many artists & musicians live up here.
How many artists have studios up here.
Dozens & dozens of artist studios are hidden
on obscure roads all through Bonny Doon.
And there are who knows how many residents
of Bonny Dooners who live hidden all along
the secret dirt & gravel roads of Bonny Doon.

                        An unassumingly
mysterious place this is—
The prominent moon rocks hill off Martin Rd.,
a party place once, sacred ground for some.
Martin Road—the Ecological Reserve pathways
of open sandy terrain of blackened skeletons
of trees of a fire that went through here in 2008
leading you into deep woods, with its secret springs
    & fern-skirted fens.
The dirt road drive to the secret lavender farm
    off Martin Rd.
The Bosch Baha'i School off Bonny Doon Rd.
The wine tasting room & pleasant garden grounds
of Beauregard Winery on Pine Flat Rd.
The hardly visible, once-in-the-past airport
    off Empire Grade.
The hairpin turns of densely wooded Ice Cream Grade.
At the north end of Empire Grade—you will see first
on the right the otherworldly lookout of Eagle Rock—,
the extremely low profile, secret military contractor
    complex of Lockheed Martin—
No one really knows what quiet black projects
    must be going on there.
Famous science fiction writer Robert Heinlein
    lived in this mysterious place.

Well-known Subconscious Comics artist Tim Eagan
    lives here.
The singer / songwriter team of Dan Frechette
    & Laurel Thompson live close by.
Artists Tessa Hope Hasty, Linda Levy, Carol Riddle,
Alison Parham, Joan Hellenthal, Suzanne Elliot,
among so many other artists yearly show their work
on studio tour weekend.
                                      And how can one
not remember the multi-patterned tiled walkways
& sculpture-towered fairyland, dotted by giant
storytelling urns, of artist Mattie Leeds.
And even mysterious lights—UFOs?—
we have heard rumors of.

The secret life of Bonny Doon is unseen
among all the trees, but it is there…
So where is Bonny Doon?

October 2020

II

Inside the Vortex
(of Santa Cruz)

2005

The Vortex

You get close enough, you start to feel it—
Oh, you're bound to feel it alright. Better keep your distance if you can't
    handle it.
The Cruz ain't no big place now, no big city, you know, everything's
kind'a compact here, so you sure feel the vibes when you're comin' in,
& when you're gettin' in real close, it's like a swirlin' sensation in the air,
& as it swirls, you feel it draw you in even more, & it'll draw you in alright—
It'll pull you—swirl you—right in.
                                          It's a spin alright, it's a dizzy-making
sort'a motion—no doubt, you'll start to go spinnin' into it yourself—
There's more rappin', more jivin', more deals bein' made, more trippin',
more losin' it, more dreamin', more schemin', more dudes dude'n it,
more strummin', more singin', more chanting, more street performin',
more oddball musicians, more tattoo rockers, more poets, more artists,
more creative cookin', more Happy Hours, more partying, more surfers,
more Peter Pans, more pagans, more feminists, more hempsters, more geeks,
more support groups, more therapists, more quantum-crazed theorists,
more wannabes, more almost-made-its, more about-to-be famous,
more once-famous, more burn-outs, more dysfunctional haven't-got-a-clue,
more bizarros, more nomads, more drifters, more time-warped hippies,
more culture junkies, more brilliant talkers, more decadent know-it-alls,
more uncommitted, more breakups, more goin' nowhere but marooned
in this town, & more lost faces, more strange names, more temptations
& more frustrations than you could find anywhere else of comparable
    geographic size—
And as you get in closer to Pacific Ave, inside the Vortex,
the swirlin' gets faster & gets more intense, it's a powerful swirlin'
    energy sink—
You get caught up in the swirl of everyone else bein' pulled in,
    you'll go spinnin' & spinnin', & spinnin' yourself—
And if you can't spin with it, it'll scatter you right out.
    It's the Vortex of The Cruz—
You never know what you'll look like comin' out the other end.

July 2003

Inside the Vortex

Within The Cruz, the Vortex, Pacific Avenue—
Have you heard about the Vortex? Have you wondered about
    the Vortex?
Shall we take a peek inside the Vortex?
            Are you prepared to peek inside the Vortex?
Will you ever be prepared in these multiple swirling currents,
   all spinning
         & spinning
                & SPINNING—

    whirling & whirling eddies of persons—

                It's the VORTEX of The CRUZ,

pulling in persons from all over places, pulling them in,
   & swirling them in—
            Inside the VORTEX,
                      inside—

You find questions, impressions, an openness & vulnerability,

    you find VIBES,
            a roiling cauldron of energies,
the craziness & chaos of a raw creative élan spitting out
momentary epiphanies of beautiful, irretrievable order—

       So precious your epiphanies—

           ***

        So you found your way here.
You've heard something about The Cruz—
Are you new in town? Passing through? Been here awhile?
   Been kickin' around for years?

Perhaps born out the Vortex itself & this all you've known—?
        (This is all but the norm to you, you think.)

Into the Vortex pulled, into the swirl of it—
Do you sense this is the place? Is this where it happens,
    out on The Edge?
Is this where you unburden yourself of all the dross of your past?
Is this where you decondition, decompress, deconstruct yourself?
    Is this where you must first fall apart?
 Is it possible this is the place where the New Life
    might be born?

        Is this the cool hip scene?

    It's *THE CRUZ*, you know

    Within The Cruz
        THE VORTEX

Inside the Vortex is a drink stronger than alcohol—
Have you drunk? How much have you drunk?

What do you find, you who would find something just for you?
Is there something here for you? There is something here for you,
    to be sure,
        there is potential here,
            there is overwhelming
                POTENTIAL—
    It is the almost-too-much.

This is the place, this is it, if you want it,
out here on The Edge of the continent—
        There is something wanting to happen here,
something wanting to manifest, to be born here—
Stand here in the swirl of the Vortex & you will feel it—
Are you prepared? Will you be? Will you ever be prepared,
    to do your part
           in the swirling birthing process?

                      Questions, questions—
You sense the swirling all around you, but can you grasp it?
Can you hold it to yourself just enough, but not to make yourself crazy,
    but to make something of it?
                                    What will you make of it?
Can you manifest it? Can you express it? Can you share it?
Is it all just too much, this spinning & swirling & whirling?
Will it scatter you out? Are you dizzy with it all?
Can you swirl with it as you hold it? Can you spin?
Can you go deeper & deeper into the whirl?

    SPIN & SPIN & SPIN

      WHIRL & WHIRL

                Did you take the drugs going round?
            Did you get snared by the jive?
              Did you get twisted by the weird?
                Are you spinning too fast?
Going round & round & not knowing when
    it will end?
Are you getting scattered out?
        You see the scattered out every day on the Ave—

There are dangers here in the swirl—
There are dangers here on the Ave.

    Will you survive this place?
    Will you find yourself anew?
        Will you thrive?
                (Don't think it's easy

There is a danger *for all of us* today,
    drawing ever so near—

            TECHNOS LOOMS

    Keep awake & keep your eyes open

Change, change, the swirl of it is all around us—
And if you can't change with it,
it can scatter you right out.
                    Or do you shut down?
Do you think this is just an interesting town?

                Most, you know,
        are oblivious to the extraordinary
            happening right smack in front of their face.

        The VORTEX—
a swirling cauldron of human energies, desires, dreams, schemes,
        & pipedreams,
& all of your everyday delusions you will find here,
                    & those rather uncommon—

            Look at all the weirdness, she said.
Hand-in-hand the young couple walks Pacific Ave—
This is The Cruz they've always heard about.

Is it the circus of characters?
Are there archetypes of persons here that grab you?
Did you come to see the street performers?
Did you come to see the spaced out, burned out, the time warped?
Did you come to see the hippies of Hippieland?
Did you come to see all the young & old Peter Pans?
Did you come to check out all the dudes & chicks?
Did you encounter the Goth? the punker? the metal head?
Did you come to see how they're all Cruz'n on The Cruz?

Are you the tourist among the streams & streams of tourists?
Did you come to browse & shop in the classy artsy shops?
Did you come for the Art, Wine & Jazz on a Sun-splashed
    of a May day?
Did you come to hang out in a café?
Are you the student among students from UC?
        Come to see a movie?
                Plenty of restaurants here—

Did you come to see the starving artists?
Did you come to cast eyes on the homeless?
What did you think?
        The homeless are here alright—
Do you have an answer for the homeless?

    Did you come to see the surfers?
        Surfers are out there, in the waters of Steamer Lane,
            you'll see the surfers *there* alright.

    Are you here to be part of the mix?

        Oh, I'm just passin' through...

Parade & parade & parade Pacific Avenue, they all do,
    you will see them all—
All are swirled in, as you are swirled in—
(& you think, you are only passing through

        Who plays the strings persons all play to?
            (Do you know about the planets?)

    SWIRL   &   SWIRL   &   SWIRL—

Was it Halloween when it all hit you?
    Was it New Years, the Town Clock?

        Is this the Avenue of Multiple Personality?
    Is this contemporary fragmentation, Postmodern town?

        What? I don't understand—

There's The Gitanos playin' in front of O'Neill,
a loud Latino gypsy sound that's gathered quite a crowd.

    There's Kuzanga's Zimbabwe marimba sound—
        the most alive intensity of a multiple heart-pumpin' beat
            around.

Perhaps you came to see the Great Morgani—
    The drift of the sound of the Great Morgani's accordion
        draws you—
            There he stands on his performer's pedestal,
his identity projecting yet another extravagant of costume—
        His face you'll never see though, not from there.

Mark is pumpin' up balloons for the kids at his usual spot,
    which he gets quite a kick out of.

Spaced out Lee is snappin' his fingers, wavin' his arms,
    rollin' his head, chantin' something Krishna.

Yes, the Umbrella Guy is here, as you might have heard,
    as if timelessly stilled in the flow,
        smiling in his full femme outfit of pink.

Remember that guy who ran for President
    from inside that cardboard box?
    He holed up here on Pacific Ave
        in a big, sign-plastered, cardboard box—
        Rumors still abound...
            Just who was that guy?

There's guitar player, one of a thousand
    who's come through here.

The Jesus leaflet people are regulars through here,
    they'll find you sooner or later.

    There's a quartet of one kind or another,
        there's a violinist,
    & she who beautifully plucked harp.

Did you ever hear that voice of the Deep South singin'?

Oh, I hear the sound of blue grass as I stroll along—

    Angel is lounging on a rug
      spread out on the pavement—
        He offers to read your cards.

       And spread out here on the pavement,
    & if not here, it'll be there, or over there—blankets
of jewelry, amulets, artsy trinkets & bric-a-brac, incense,
    booklets of some kind...
        oh, patchouli you'll get a waft of
      somewhere in the air...

   Did you ever see the Magic Man perform
     at his little magic table?

   Did you ever see the Bubble Gique?
     His most enormous of bubbles you will ever see.

  The juggler guy, now he makes it look
all so effortless—glass balls roll
    like crystal water flowing
      & never loses a drop.

  The break-dancers this Saturday afternoon
    I would have to say are as good as they get.

   The Night Out drumming, on & on & on it went,
      induced altered states that September evening.

   Ever see the salsa dancers in front of the Palomar?

Did you ever see Art & Revolution playfully mock the Machine?
  Or the Bare-Breasted Bandits do their protest thing?

      In the flow of it all
they're talkin' on their cell phones—

He's talkin' on his cell phone,
& directly across the street, there's another,
talkin' on his cell phone,
& there's another, & another—
a couple's walkin' by each on a cell phone...

TECHNOS LOOMS

                In the parking lot behind Logos
you find our surrealist poet Erich stabbing about in the dark—
Do not assume anything.

           Were you ever kissed on the Avenue?
She came up & kissed me & didn't even know me,
but somehow she must have known my birthday was the epitome
   of synchronicity—

      Did you ever march down the old Mall?
      Do you remember the old Mall?
            —Pacific Garden Mall?
      (Before the Quake, you know)
      Did you ever protest something or another?
       Ever carry your banner of Pride?
          Or was it a banner, *Freeze the Nukes*,
        or *Stop Star Wars?*

Remember Kosmic Lady who carried her cross
     on the old Mall?
          She knew the signs—
She told us the Space People were here.

   A group of us modeled our ET t-shirts that time,
       the camcorder rolled, all the spectators gawked,
         something was happening here...

   Here we go—

SWIRL & SWIRL & SWIRL

SPIN & SPIN

faster & faster & further & further we go in—

Who can grasp what untamed, unforeseen, roiling & thick & potent
    creative brew
        swirls & swirls here
                in the very center of the Vortex Pacific Avenue?
Who can fathom what deeper & deeper inner process works
    in the faster & faster swirl of it all?
What Vision to Fountain forth in a firework of epiphanies—

        Precious seeds your epiphanies!
           You who live a life of epiphanies—

        They keep swirling in alright.

          It's a spin alright—

Did you get your impression? get an insight? perhaps a little excite-
    ment?
Were you amused? Was it all so cool?
               Or the germ of something grand?

          This is PSYCHE's Cauldron,
          I've been given to understand.

        (& I have given you a clue

      How energy has a spin to it—
      The little quasi-particles spin,
      they spin & spin alright—

        What spinning ball
           out of the spin of the Vortex
        will you be
                for all to see?

What spinning, swirling currents of persons out of this beautiful
   crazy place
              go out
                      to all directions of the world—?
Are you the artist going out to the world?
Are you the writer of that maverick book?
Are you that street poet from Oklahoma, come & gone?
Are you the world-acclaimed dancer?
Are you the UC professor with a worldwide reputation?
Are you that soul singer with the big bold voice?
Are you the folksinger who's kicked around here for years?
Are you that famous Bubble Maker, bringing your bubble magic
   to all the world?
Are you the filmmaker? The videographer of documentaries?
Did you write the screenplay for that movie we all saw?
Do you have a screenplay you think will make it big?
Are you the publishers behind that monthly?
Are the the herbalist behind all those original formulations?
Did you have a band once that got around on the circuit?
Are you that Postmodern-styled neopagan astrologer?
Are you the one we saw on that TV program?
Are you the cyber wizard? The computer graphics artist?
Are you the psychic? The one who channeled various entities?

                I did hint once, didn't I,
                there's a new fish up there
                in the sky
                where the Moon is.

    (Was I not the Multi Guy on Pacific Ave?

You better open your eyes though—

                TECHNOS LOOMS

      From Silicon Valley TECHNOS LOOMS

    Postmodern, *what?*

I said, It's quite the Postmodern place to be, you know,
but it's all a transition to—

What did you expect?
    Did you take it all in?

Is this the culture mulch? Is this the new soil?

Inside the Vortex,
    did you have a Vision?

Did you see the Fountain?

    Did you see the Tree rising out of the Fountain?

    Did you hear the Tree singing?

***

Into the VORTEX

    inside the VORTEX

    out of the VORTEX

the eddies of persons form & dissolve...

    What wild, beautiful thing has been born here
    to answer the Age?

What Vision to confront TECHNOS?

    Is there a singing to confront TECHNOS?

Is there a Melody
    out of the confused medley
    of the VORTEX
        to turn the ear of TECHNOS?

What part do you play?
What Vision do *you* bring to the world
   from out of this place?

   This place of the

      SWIRL & SWIRL & SWIRL

         SPIN & SPIN

         WHIRL & WHIRL

      The VORTEX of The CRUZ

November-December 2005

III

*The Cruz
& other poems*

1988-1990 / 2016

The Cruz

I saw the Dance She was,
but how was I to join the Dance She was?

Follow me, She said, *Take my lead.*
I will show you death & I will show you resurrection.
I am The Cruz.   I destroy & some I raise.

And She is seductive & beautiful, unhesitating & cruel,
She is untouchable but lust rapturous, & how my 26 years
    I sacrificed—
I found myself poised upon Her bleached-bone cliffs,
Her teeth-carved & claw-marked, ocean-savaged cliffs,
its rocks littered by dream skulls of thousands,
    abandoned at the American Edge.

I am The Cruz.   I am what you seek.

                                    And so I sought
the Love I lost, only short months after arriving The Cruz—
Two of us, from the Midwest, had arrived one day this place The Cruz,
we had come to The Edge, uncertain & hopeful, ready to take any plunge—
She was a young Master of Love, but too late, I realized, too late—
    already, overnight, she left for someone new—
She burst out her sudden, I-never-imagined *Good-bye* & tears filled
my car & tears met strangers for weeks on streets & in bars, until tears
    were no more.
And so *I* was seduced, by someone new—
I stood before Her deep Bay body & saw Her night shimmering waters
    of Moon
             below—
I saw the descent She was & so I surrendered—I took the plunge—,
& so I went down—I gave myself to Her, descended into Her,
& into the labyrinthine corridors of Her I followed Her—
I followed Her willing & persistent where the Western river emptied
    its lost mind onto the Mall, where the nation's money crisp tourists

    & weekend escapees were alarmed & amazed & annoyed & oblivious
        to the shards of reality disintegration flying at their faces, & weeping
        ghost bodies around them were multiplying.
I followed Her where street punks & skin heads marauded & shifted
        among rudiments of primal gesture & guitar sirens wailed rifts
        of apocalyptic message transmitted from heavens of radio.
I followed Her where evangels still dragged their medieval chains
        & dopers blown out by precocious Sixties psychedelia fantasia
        foraged on Postmodern broken pavement, & crazies & freaks
        of America's dark asylum tide of future mass mind schizophrenia
        poured from Her floodgates, inundating the calloused streets.
I followed Her through carnival of Krishna chants & tinkling bells,
        of dancing Rajneesh devotees & daredevil skateboarders,
        of sidewalk jugglers & salvation petitioners, of UFO Noahs,
        streetwise cons & cemetery trolls, of backpack cowboy drifters
        & the local vigilantes, headbuster surfers & rednecks.
I followed Her where office workers outside ate lunch on benches
        & watched helpless at this last outpost of Western decline,
        where the invisible cry from the abandoned doorway rang out,
        Spare change for the strange! Spare change for the strange!
I followed Her into eyes of women pushing baby & worrying if sky
        brought bread or warhead brimstone, & women who held hands
        of five-year-olds were asking, *Is there a next daddy?*
I followed Her, my let loose release of heart raving on Irish coffee high
        screaming at the platinum Moon that lonesome midnight, silent
        storefront windows reverberating, I was without her, I was
        without her, & how I needed her.
I followed Her & said, *So this is it, this is where I must be delivered over,*
        where I must be dismembered & must die, where I must relinquish
        all past observances of universe conditioning.
I followed Her nightly & jobless, a year of food stamps & survival,
        but five minutes to a donut shop where a public office I set up
        & serviced student curiosity, depression, exam crises & hormone
        palpitations & hoping always the next one walking in was her.
I followed Her nightly & all the street penny poor streamed in the sugar
        & caffeine oasis, & campers & squatters from up the coast furnished
        guitar & song & Tom the Bubble Man performed his bubble magic

    for us all, & her eyes across the counter questioned my intentions,
       her eyes of women's studies, her eyes blinking from Bethany Bible
       College, her green graphic eyes from Sacramento—we talked,
       might see you sometime, she vanished into never.
I followed Her & she told me with a big-cheeked bent tooth smile
       of a soul-fated infatuation, its progress daily, a man partially
       imaginary, yet she loved him nonetheless & I understood.
I followed Her to the pot haze, beer piss & hard drunk, cocaine
       in the back room, endless yearlong circuit of parties, of party town
       weekends, birthdays, holidays, post-exam post-semester bashes,
       between quarter bashes, nightly summer debauches, theme parties,
       costume parties & *You can come as you are, you madman,* & always,
       Would I find her tonight?
I followed Her & danced orgiastic & incantations spouted & raved
       monologue improvisations while Lowell & Pound & Eliot students
       sideways leaned & stared, dumbfounded by what they saw,
       mouths watering for a taste of real life, & I laughed & planted
       the Muse's flowers in lamp shades & curtains.
I followed Her spinning, dancing on heads, a bacchanalian whirl
       sweeping through us all, where one by one fell away & collapsed
       into sleep, & across a wall her unleashed body her arms I splayed
       & one immortal kiss we kissed before I too fell away & ended
       in a neighborhood ditch hiatus of consciousness, & hours later
       stumbled upon syllables before the wine-sick dawn toward home,
       & days later she confessed, she was a simple-hearted Catholic
       frightened by Dionysus.
So I followed Her to all the wharf's trinket, tee shirt & poster shops,
       where she left a trail of Midwestern fingerprints & tourists snapshot
       Her body without knowing & the belly of the Boardwalk Cartesian
       dichotomized masses bloated on junk food & processed fun,
       where I stood with her among gulls, fish lines & sea lions
       & the sons & daughters of America & saw visions of Goddess
       rise from the Bay & learned patience, patience—
O once we talked quietly gazing upon the calm powder blue 4th of July
       phantom Navy ship lit waters & all was mystery & enchantment.
I followed Her to City on a Hill Birth of a Poet meditation rituals,
       all the young ears I saw entranced by the Voice, where Helen

    invited me into the poet's private tornado & the lightning finger
        accusation boomed at me: I dare come with golden Helen
        & disrupt the old poet's concentration?
I followed Her & flirted always dangerously with the ever fuse-lit
        femme fatale, but I was dense that once—*Wait for me,* she said
        that night, she left for dinner with another guy, *I'll be back later*—
        through my hesitant fingers she slipped—I didn't wait—
        & born that day was the child regret, & I regret.
I followed Her a bridesmaid, when Mat & I a wedding ritual performed
        written for a Detroit comrade one unexpected rainy September
        campus day & I sent her foolish letters & I walked out upon
        the world hillside, the panorama of Her beautiful opened
        oceanic arms & thighs calling:

Sacrifice your life to me & I will show you wonders.

So I followed Her to Caffé Purgatory where life story recitals
        were given daily & I fostered my espresso delirium with notebook
        & pen & nostalgia for memories warm flooded my veins & waves
        came over of sorrow & compassion for the failed & wasted
        & blown out & burned out & spaced out & would-bes
        at every table, somehow to redeem.
I followed Her & I was Vision pregnant biding my time preparation,
        as local nerd-brains sat hunched & flaunted their whispers
        of high-tech intelligentsia takeover & perennial student combatants
        read their Marx, Nietzsche, Derrida, Freud, Foucault & Adorno,
        made mincemeat sandwich critiques of all newcomers daily,
        & from a distance I saw her wink.
I followed Her that night to the Purg & listened to her short-term
        breakup with boyfriend confession, & so we bar hopped for drinks
        & we exchanged our woeful tales of struggle, frustration & trials,
        & phone numbers we exchanged, & our trysts were my first,
        & I followed where I never did meet again the *Tropic of Cancer*
        inquisitive young soul.
I followed Her still to Halloween bongos of another time & place
        & searched for her among a thousand phantasmagoric masks
        & what she offered after drinks turned out a wrong number,
        she said she was frightened that night of Dionysus when later
        we dated— O that freer & more expressive time when Sylvia,

femme fatale extraordinaire, sauntered in the café threshold
& stood coquettish so all could adore her, & upon hearing
my Muse she rushed up & gnawed on my arm in a frenzy.
I followed Her into the attic of poets with no money for rent
& how I survived a year like that was a wonder, She was
destroying me…& friend Bill climbed the ladder visiting me
with poems, & street poet Jim & Goddess obsessed Sylvia
each did their stints in the roof, & one evening I dragged
her out the Four Square Church, her curiosity a Pandora's box,
dinner was ready, I said.
I followed Her to nightclubs The Catalyst, Edgewater, Vets Hall
& Wooden Nickel, O.T.'s, Civic, Dream Inn, old Thatcher's
upstairs & Dragon Moon manic nonstop disco dervish dancing,
& was swept into punk, new wave Batteries, Humans, Tao
Chemical slam dancing craze, where we shared desire glances,
sly thigh caresses & kissed in frantic whipped up heat
& embraced for another one night, in a beginning trail
of one nights.
Yes, I followed Her through pickup markets of lust & yearning
& frustration, where my first birthday present that night
invited me home & I got giddy & nervous & said maybe later,
& later my second sat on a bar stool & this one *I* invited home,
but she again was afraid that night of Dionysus after foreplay
undress, & soon the mid-Eighties AIDS paranoia imprisonment
of the joy of sex began.
I followed Her despairing I was not a 50-thousand-a-year man, nor a 40,
nor a 30, not even a 20—those eunuch-making eyes she flashed
expecting Mr. Money & not, O God, another dog-starved writer!
I followed Her the difficult one two years with paychecks I couldn't
pour fast enough into her drinks & flowers, chocolates & steaks,
but the consummate act postponed, until that night in her proper
dustfree apartment we downed two bottles of wine & I unveiled her.
I followed Her to Pearl Alley Bistro & sat snapping fingers at impossible
daydreaming women romancing specters of always some impossible
Mr. Right swimming in a wine glass, & they returned home each one
to beds of No-man's-land.
I followed Her to hospital duty, six years a witness of DOA & Code 99
automobile & motorcycle gruesome mangled & crumpled up bodies,
of bones grinding, limbs mashed, skulls cracked, gunshots, slashings,

of eyes floating in bloody sockets, & chest tubes stuck out the poor
   woman…& I numbered her bruises after her boyfriend beat her
   & left her—she invited me to come later to see for myself.
I followed Her injecting impromptu poetry stimulants into ER lazy hours
   & PBX operator was serenaded between incoming calls, & I was the
   talk down—nurse made me—counselor of drunks, dopers, suicidal
   souls comforting & was the get down leather restrainer of PCP, acid,
   & alcohol writhing berserkos, & all the schizos who heard me speak
   knew *my* language & wished me luck.
I followed Her a double life dating nurses, techs, housekeepers & clerks,
   my dark Pluto clouded years of flirtations & crushes & infatuations
   & with Carolyn love to addiction—How far can you go, foolish you?—
   & polite rejections & *Can you come out & look at my car, It won't start*,
   the nurse winked, & secret hallway kisses, & I followed Her
   into dim lit rooms & her eyes spoke of oceans & I would drown,
   & I met the mother from lost Lemuria visiting her broken-leg son
   & I brought home & we embraced, in another of one nights.
I followed Her into backyard cabins & tents & redwood groves,
   into garages & artist studios, & followed her home for kisses
   when she said *Proust*, & around the beach bonfire the future
   New Age bard opened up vistas for her & her friends…
   & how often Michael at Toots wondered of the fish I brought up
   from the sea, we walk in hand-in-hand & I make introductions.
I followed Her my dear friend Jan at my feet on the beach,
   she was assertive with come-ons & lips & I cold & abstract
   began to explain why from certain women I held back
         —O sing the torments of Aphrodite!—
   & so we sat & sipped at The Catalyst & analyzed enlightened
   our expectations, desires, the mystery of attraction, our different
   styles, & still she was willing to cozy up, whatever favor I asked,
   together we cuddled back in my cave.
I followed Her & agonized when she asked *me* out, she was lonely
   & looking & cooked for me & dressed for me & wore the lipstick
   I liked & smothered me with such eyes of mothering, But why?
   I asked, Why was she never the right one? the one *I* wanted?
         —O cruel wiles of Aphrodite!—
   & so I discovered again my turn to say *Sorry*.

O I followed Her into nights of my cold-floor studio solitary bed
of private invocations of Her name & She the succubus came
answering my plea:

If you will let me destroy you, I will take you higher.

So I followed Her from the bus & she led me to the Guru Mahari ji
encounter, beautiful & brittle sweet she was, the sweetest voice,
where she sat facing us an exhibitionist shameless with testimony,
sharing her guru-induced orgasm gushing with such confessions
& epiphanies & hot endearments.
I followed Her to Phoenix New Age Coffeehouse of incense atmosphere
& such ethereal metaphysical music highs—no bad vibes allowed here—
where the Supreme Masters' pictures smiled upon us & angels sang
from above, & I peeked in & eavesdropped on groupie pep talks
—the budding local guru spoke in the backroom—, & she walked in
dressed a saintly phantom of flowing white, wafted by Spirit,
her feet hovering inches off the ground…she touched ground later
in my bedroom & lay willing before me.
I followed Her to visualization, meditation, crystal, tarot, numerology,
astrology, hugs & hand holding & chanting workshops & gatherings
& so many café consultations & over the phone what's your sign
& what planets were transiting, she the type to worry about money
& career while ascending the higher planes of inner being,
or too vegetarian gentle she was for the radical matter-enmeshed artist
I was, & often her soft serious voice questioned me about spiritual
credentials.
I followed Her unbelieving when she said romance was dead meat,
the heart a shriveled, dried-up clot, or when she led me into woods
& private worlds only to admit, *Sorry, I'm not very romantic these days,*
shrinking from my kiss, & a week later I spy her on the street
with the new short-term love of her life.
I followed Her through a year of feminist ideology & constant critique
of my ways, LA-San Fran art circuit travels & long-welcomed,
always-the-right-time lovemaking, O the spontaneous lust fire
I thrived on! like the days of my Master, & lips willing to utter
ecstatic poesy embracing at the surf!

I followed Her the artist through twisting corridors on land, air & sea,
    she led me to conferences, movies & receptions & New Mexican
    lands of pueblos & desert, & I her thesis advisor & other feminists
    were always suspicious & wary…& dare I perform that night
    a ritual for Goddess liberation? —I dared, dressed black as night.
I followed Her & one day we stood atop the world upon Loma Prieta
    & beheld the four directions & below us lay The Cruz beautiful
    & bizarre we both agreed, the day Lilian received her summons—
    her Muse called her to the distant Sun of the desert, she saying
    this Cruz was suicide, but I would not & could not abandon,
    no, not yet, & so *Good-bye,* & lonely were the love-lacking days
    I counted & counted again.
So I followed Her again through yearlong calendars marked up
    with new rendezvous: bookstores, cafés, bars, pubs, restaurants,
    hospital parking lot 6 am, we go out & have breakfast.
I followed Her to video stores & VCR living rooms, to movie theatres,
    readings, openings, performances, weekly happy hour all over town,
    & I cooked dinner for her, & 4:30 in the afternoon we always met,
    on duty I was—a security clearance I had—working in high-techville
    Scotts Valley…& I improved her compositions & helped sharpen
    her poetry.
I followed Her & her peace & political conscience, in service to her,
    a Nuclear Weapons Freeze volunteer, I answered her call,
    sitting on steering committee, gopher in office, on the Mall tabling,
    at shopping centers, fairs & dances, & we marched through town
    & proudly displayed banner *Test Ban Treaty,* & two years
    a staff writer for our local *Monthly Planet* I was spreading flames
    of our nuclear discontent, & we warned Earth of the coming
    Star Wars menace.
I followed Her & practiced political correctness—but never in heart
    space did we meet—the New Age Vision the poet again & again
    offered was always axed from priority action agendas, politics
    & Dionysus no mix in cheerless 80s humdrum stagnation.
I followed Her through innumerable close encounters, psychic platonic
    connections, the mutual mind charge, & *This is getting dangerous,*
    Let's be friends, she wanted only a part of me, not really all of me,
    & so I discovered again her fear of commitment, once again
    those cold fish feet.

I followed Her & how close we would come, I would lie next to her,
   arms wrapped around her, all love sap drippy, & she casual listened
   to radio desire these syrupy of romance songs & distant fantasized
   someone other—I can still see Maureen's wistful dreamland eyes
   —or MTV torsos gyrated as we watched from her couch
   & how I fondled her.
I followed Her through phone calls of seduction, complications,
   triangles, innuendos, beginner psychoanalysis & the truth
   came out, Is it me or him? welling up in anger & recriminations,
   & I grieved, after my having said *Good-bye,* but didn't mean it,
   I never mean it, she hung up & then called back.
I followed Her & discovered what is a friend: *A friend,* Mindy said,
   when I drove her to work, & I will never forget, we will never
   let each other go, overcoming all expectations, jealousy & hurt,
   our threads are entwined for a future in friendship goes before us.
I followed Her to LA, Laguna Beach, San Fran, Big Sur, back & forth
   San Jose, New Mexico, Sonoma, Colorado, Amtrak cross country,
   & her postcards & letters I received, Why was she always leaving?
   —for LA, for San Francisco, for Sonoma, Santa Fe, Boston,
   New York, Washington, Iowa, Illinois, for home state Michigan.
I followed Her in Sylvia's car, visiting her in breakdown Southland
   hospital—they took her gun away & locked her up awhile,
   I consulted with her psychiatrist—& in Lilian's car nightly, going
   to work Watsonville & babysat in day her five-year-old Rambo,
   & followed Her in Cathy's car a whole year I used—she couldn't
   drive anyway—, & finally, in my own car, I drove her everywhere,
   thanking her profusely for the years she helped me.
I followed Her through an endless loop of conversations with all
   my baffled, unattached friends, & it was always the questions,
   *What is it with The Cruz? What curse upon it? What crazy energy?
   What a disaster this place! This rubbish heap of shattered relationships
   & shattered lives!*
I followed Her & her transitions, crises, tears & confusions, I was
   always the companion & confidant of soul, helping her through
   her trials & offering her the Fire & Water of alchemical renewal,
   helping her to tell her Story, so often she stuttered, could not
   explain, found herself in panic in the Labyrinth of the Age.

I followed Her word by word through the dreary 80s litany she tried
    over & over to get out of her mind: *Life is tough & Life is hard.*
    No time for love. No time for Dionysus. But never, I said,
    Never would I resign myself in hopelessness.
I followed Her faithfully even as I despaired again & again fate
    would not allow me to find the right woman at the right time.
I followed Her faithfully & she who searched for me never saw me,
    the Invisible Man.
I followed Her through these Teflon years, this passion-shackled,
    nuclear-gagged & frightened time, this confused blot
    of whacked-out & cynical time that now finally & fatefully
    has conceived, a Vision of a child born of the Creative Divine.

I followed Her in search of Her,
    always agonizing & asking,
How long must I suffer this Cruz?
How long can I go on? What fate is this?
only to be dismembered by Her hands,
I howled to be destroyed by Her—

    If you would be my poet,
    I must destroy you first.

Was I to abandon The Cruz? When the secret
of Divine Love through suffering my search
I was discovering?
              On the streets the story goes—
I've been on The Cruz before & once already escaped.
Two years on The Cruz & you're lucky you've survived.
Escape The Cruz, they said, *such a search will destroy you—*

For She destroys & I saw how each She destroys differently—
Destroys first-book successful writer six months on The Cruz,
    ambitions sucked out by straw as she lounges in the Sun.
Destroys PR queen who flew north from LA on wings of her Muse,
    ultimate groupie, too much acid & fantasies of fast lane,
    her breakdown in crisis center & *I am lost, I am a reprobate*
    I heard over & over, driving her rented car through
    soul tunnel in hell, watching her burn next to me.

Destroys by the perpetual raining down from Neptune clouds coke,
    smack, weed, acid, angel dust, ludes, meth & downers & all
    the eager hands reach out & whole inheritances & trust funds
    are wiped out, one-third salaries sacrificed, jobs lost, families ruined,
    minds scrambled, tubes forced through noses nightly at the hospital.
Destroys the tie-dyed, left-over of Sixties hippies & homeless squatters
    of pavements, waiting & waiting for the never-to-come Sixties
    revival, now it's the late 80s & they're still on The Edge hangin' on
    & trippin' in their own time warps.
Destroys the ego bubble of surrealist poet, his grandiose visions
    of Rimbaud, wizard of going out too far & dope schizophrenic
    death.
Destroys couples flocking in search for the hope-filled promise
    of new life, only to find devilish spirits out of the mountains
    invading their moments, & repressions, resentments, frustrations
    erupt, & hundreds of temptations walk the streets every day,
    & they break up.
Destroys high school grads grown up on TV pop decadence,
    their fragmented brain discs overloaded, rootless scavengers
    loose on the streets, or resigned & cynical of Technos career,
    the only future offered.
Destroys scores of UC grads who linger in ever seductive laid-back town,
    for years floundering, drifting, forever daydreaming that some sign
    out of the heavens would be given them.
Destroys through the constant whirlwind of extroversion madness,
    always the coming & going of parties, receptions & spider web
    networks of friends, nonstop caught, accomplishing nothing,
    all becomes a blur.
Destroys hundreds of hole-in-the-wall artists & writers & poets
    who hang out in town every day, all competing for crumbs fallen
    from media tables of public attention, eyeing each other, ignoring
    each other, Postmodern epigones out on a hopeless Cruz,
    always it's old news.
Destroys those who once had a guru-knows-all & now are left to fend
    for themselves perplexed in the profound muck of the material plane,
    they peer into existential zero.
Destroys those slaving to pay higher & higher bills in beautiful playland
    Cruz, the slow worm of bitterness & regret eating at them, lost are all
    the fun opportunities, & wives & husbands can't take it, they leave.

Destroys the multi-talented so sensitive man utterly incapable of asserting,
   acting, taking a stand in the ever-changing emotional weather,
   he sits wondrous passive daily at the café.
Destroys those in marriages of silent desperation, birds of her imagination
   falling dead in their cage, at the party she hints how many already,
   Who could help save the others?
Destroys marriages over discoveries of secret lovers he & she cannot
   do without, obsessed & greedy for this thing called love.
Destroys him soliciting me to help him buy vodka as he peruses tables
   at the Caméléon, I listen to his sighs & moans of missed & wasted
   opportunities, his regrets & envy of the hangout students he attaches
   himself to.
Destroys her getting unexpected pregnant after the thrill of her new town
   high, & now her future is baby's survival.
Destroys the old beat poet smacked out with boxes of manuscripts piled
   around him in St. George Hotel room, he warns me of hell just ahead.
Destroys the occult Messiah out of the north, can't find followers, he sits
   on a bench on the Mall, pines for his ancient priestly power.
Destroys the Heidegger scholar now zombie on the streets, he walks by
   mouthing monophraseology of Dasein & Being.
Destroys her with a bullet to the face after kinky cocaine insane rituals
   & accusation jealousies.
Destroys the 16-year-olds out drinking, they lose control & smash up,
   their beer bottles found in the car at bottom of the cliff, their friend
   is dead.
Destroys those tempting the thunderous breakers out on the rocks,
   swept away monstrously by the storm.
Destroys him scoffing at the Here & Now of living Passion one day
   at the café, then went to hang himself.
Destroys those on a quest clueless in the Labyrinth, the Minotaur
   of madness slowly rips them to shreds.

She destroys. And a hundred, a thousand times,
through eyes & smiles & kisses & intimacies
when I offered myself only to lose Her again & again,
She destroyed me, but my discovery of Divine Love
      She could not destroy.

You who dared destruction—
No man has followed me as you have followed me.
With Divine Love discovered, follow me & know me embodied.

And I followed Her still—
& I know Her, the fish who sold flowers, who swam through
    department store waving arms.
I know Her, pot spaced TV catatonic staring at the boob screen
    for hours, she can name the stars by heart.
I know Her, cigarette pouting brat always gets her way, impatient
    for someone to get on with fame.
I know Her, homeless mom & two-year-old we took in, years later
    she silently glides by.
I know Her, Kosmic Lady, sending me UFO letters & postcards
    of splintered prophecy.
I know Her, jock woman, wanted to teach me surfing: *Are you afraid*
    of the ocean?
I know Her, Susanna Banana running stop signs, her big little girl eyes
    smiling at me.
I know Her, 4th one on the right, broccoli trim line Watsonville,
    we exchange language barrier mispronounced words.
I know Her, the space cadets who rubbed my back & cooed soothingly,
    This life is illusion, Let us play.
I know Her, 17-year-old Catalyst butterfly who always managed to flit by
    the bouncers.
I know Her, renting room with teenage punk son, wanting me to listen
    to Eno through new *Walkman* earphones.
I know Her, the Lioness, ravishing her feminist man for another round
    of good time.
I know Her, Black Widow, will toy with you until her poison paralyzes.
I know Her, always driving away, my last kiss on her lips.
I know Her, still married, & I'm afraid her husband might kill me.
I know Her, insanely possessive & jealous, who slams doors & screams,
    who curses & smashes & punches in your face.
I know Her, long, silk-haired, cool Santa Cruz girls who wanna have fun
    with the boys hot with beer in their balls.
I know Her, sweet café honey, attracted men like flies & hung them
    & named them in her secret menagerie.
I know Her, another artist hopeful, too young yet to be destroyed.

I know Her, artist of some accomplishment, destroyed already
 & patiently awaiting a new inspiration.
I know Her, the hyperactive do-gooder of a thousand friends.
I know Her, Edgewater dancer whose Christ portrait shed real tears,
 the priests hushed it up.
I know Her, trying to finish her novel, shrewdly plotting her every
 occupational move meanwhile to survive.
I know Her, still carrying around all her childhood stuff, burdened
 with perpetual hurt for life.
I know Her, frightened one with a Bible & loaded gun in her purse,
 in the theatre she shows me as we wait for the movie.
I know Her, androgynous in leather jacket & slicked-back hair.
I know Her, Working Girl, jumps into cars & names her price.
I know Her, Snow Queen, keeping me up all night with an endless
 life story & models for me her million-dollar wardrobe.
I know Her, mother of pyramids & crystals, thinks her 19-year-old son
 is a new generation square.
I know Her, rarely seen, home ridden with her secret anorexic obsession.
I know Her, still virgin, boasting having dated over one hundred men,
 & I too couldn't provide the right password.
I know Her, Ms. Constant Tangent who gleefully threw off her clothes
 to dance more freely before students at concert UC.
I know Her, Ms. Take Charge, brings along her two pair handcuffs
 for extended play.
I know Her, Desperate to Marry, time to abandon The Cruz,
 move East to family commitment, better luck land.
I know Her, Mind Made Up, time to move to Silicon Valley,
 get Technos good pay job.
I know Her, getting burned again, but not by me.
I know Her, date with the bedroom boyfriend, you only find out later.
I know Her, all over town, dozens of well-wishing waitresses.
I know Her, 20 candles flickering in her private museum bedroom,
 cold January night.
I know Her, ever searching, designed flow charts of her entire life
 & still came up lost.
I know Her, once green-haired leathered punk, now in sharp tie
 officer uniform.
I know Her, Ms. Radical Fem, who proudly bared her breasts
 to the city.

I know Her, eccentric thinker, brilliant recluse in her house full
    of inventions, diagrams, blueprints & journals.
I know Her, quitting secretary job, wants to study in the mountains
    shaman medicine.
I know Her, nurse with the pickup & backpack always leaving,
anywhere but here, never settles down.
I know Her, mother of four, watching daily her husband demolish
    & rebuild their home bigger than ever.
I know Her, In Service to God, wanted me to tell her a Story,
    a new visionary truly divine-inspired Story.
I know Her, Master of Love I was once blessed with & lost.

But I found. The Story of another Love has begun.
What Love is this? A Love greater still? Is it possible?
That I, suffering all, could still love them all
& love each story, for a Love I could not find,
through Her I found, who is Master Divine.
I say the stories of all will someday
be woven into the great Story *of* all.
This is the Story behind the stories of all—
This is the Story beginning, revelation
of Goddess of this place & time.
This is the Story I now set myself to tell,
Vision of a child born of the Creative Divine,
    my Love for Psyche Divine...

So you found me in manifestation.
Into my Dance I led you & in my Dance
I crushed, pulverized & melted you,
separated your elements & distilled you.
Yet does Love persist? Not destroyed?
Know then, I have refined you & resurrected you,
a Selfhood unpredicted, unfathomed, plutonium potent.
You are more powerful than any warhead of the nations.

I raise you from the rubbish heap & ashes.
Stand at the threshold of a New Age
& prepare all for my world-shattering & resurrecting Vision.
For I resurrect.   I create.   I nurture.   I am the Fountain
of a Creativity as of yet unimagined.   I am The Cruz
     & I am The Rose.

I saw: Saw Her at the American Edge testing souls,
Her golden veil drawing thousands, preparing mulch
for the new tilling of the Ages, that here new Vision
     could be planted,
& from this most bizarre & perplexing & difficult
& beautiful & powerful place, the Tree of New Self
     could rise.

I learned the Dance She was,
I entered the Dance of death She was,
but in Her Fountain I rose & rose anew—
Holy this place, The Cruz,
Holy Cross, Santa Cruz—

Santa Cruz
Nov. 14 – Dec. 15, 1988
2016

Caffé Pergolesi

Cast forth, or simply stepping out from the world,
they arrive & settle in & often rearrange themselves,
suspended in time at tables & benches;
       & inside the red brick vault
more line up & await their fix.
Peeking from ivy, high above, *Caffé Pergolesi*
in Gothic bronze

      greets

      the arrivals

           And they come,
all the daylong laid back, the hanger-outers,
all the students & artists & ol' dropout hippies—
They come, all the nightly dopers & bizarros
& street walkin' schizos & burnouts, & the politicos—
They come, all the punkers & new wave hip—

With bio & psych & computer texts in hand,
novels cracked open, newspapers piled, notepads scribbled in
& *Village Voice* taken from racks, with school compositions spread,
& postcards to send & letters back home to send,
                they come—

They come, all the one-time tourists & everyday regulars
   & just cruzin' through—
They come, all the techies & yuppies amidst the street livin'
of homeless mothers & fathers & backpack drifters
   & wanderers—
They come, all the losers, posers & pretenders,
all the naive hopefuls & would-bes & wannabes & seekers
   & survivors & the perpetually struggling—
And university physicists hunch close playing chess,
& musicians set up & strike up the inspired bright chords
   of Renaissance—

They come, all the people watchers themselves watched
    & accountable—
And who is not accountable? We all must act, must act
    in the world.
                And all tell stories—

They come, from Connecticut & Washington, Canada, France,
New York, Switzerland, Denver, Chicago, Detroit, Texas,
Japan, England, Germany, Mexico, Hawaii, Jamaica,
    from LA, Berkeley & San Fran.

It's the endless shuffle
of cups & glasses lined up, scattered & retrieved—
The fix: coffees, cappuccinos, espressos, lattes,
    cocoas, sodas & teas.
And the lone ceiling fan spins & sways in a leisurely
    dream atmosphere—
And I have come for weeks & months & years.
I have sat & listened.
I have heard them all...

To purge

        In the corner sits street poet Jim
        sipping espresso, like precious elixir,
        to inspire
        to catch
        the ol' beat poet rhythm—
        Old beatnik dreams live on.
        Keep the flame alive.
        Does his routine for quarters & dimes
        & sweet greenbacks & all the sweet smiles
            he can get—
        Dude, you wanna hear my latest?

It's a long road from Oklahoma,
longer yet to try to make it.

            To purge the soul

And onto the terrace saunters LA Sylvia,
she lingers in the doorway, big notebook flat
against her chest,
                      she pans the tables—

Do they see her? Will they notice?
A man picked up a day ago tags after,
Sylvia always the attention getter,
restless, flirtatious, a people consumer—
Her specialty: PR for any rising star

            Hello, Sylvia,
            I say—

& Branden & Ken zero in, critique her maneuvers,
ambassadors in the American wasteland of French intelligence,
pacing themselves through Derrida, Foucault & Barthes,
Deleuze & Lacan, thick blue smoke of Gauloises
swirling among the dance of their sentences—
Their psychoanalytical observations are peppered
with smirks & chuckles, how the local artists entertain them,
their stories/case histories
                        of critique
                        as I in the baptism
                        of critique
survived
at the hands of
these self-styled Nietzschean nomads
in this decadent disoriented late 20th Century cultureland.

                    perennial students
                    no other life worthwhile
                    but read & party day in/day out

& Maureen brings friends from Boston visiting,
they sample the scene, in proper conservative casual;
I flit back & forth, making small talk with them,
    Maureen is uneasy—
Who are those weirdos? she high-strung nervous asks.
To think, I once had such a crush on her—

They come, all the weirdos, decadents & nihilist intellectuals,
all the crazies, hopeless dreamers & street corner prophets...

& the group recoups from last night's debauch,
tonight they'll start again—
   hard booze, speed, pot, cocaine & acid...

& Branden goes days livin' on noodles & coffee,
it's remarkable the drugs don't faze him,
brilliant sentences yet stream from his tongue,
a contemporary sophist in New Age Athens...

& young Scott zips through *Being and Time,*
consumed & tossed aside

     & destruction is all around

of metaphysics
the ruins of lives
ruins of culture
perfect opportunities
for scavengers & pirates...

& beyond the mountains, superpowers up the ante
for nuclear Armageddon...

     more fighting
     in Lebanon
     Iran/Iraq
     Nicaragua
     El Salvador

& the rain forests are disappearing
thousands of Earth species disappearing
more chemical spills/oil spills
Chernobyl spewing radioactivity...

& cafe sophists argue harmlessly
about the harmless fascists among them...

& endless the rendezvous of friends, endless dates & trysts,
endless weaving of stories, endless hours dribbling away,
idle chitchat, snippets of gossip/autobiography
in easy laid-back town…

                        & Lilian visits,
                        we sit on the terrace,
                        six years ago we were lovers—
                        She's in New Mexico now,
                        tells me of her new life & art,
                        a feminist,
                        on her way up…

& Margaret & Mindy from the hospital
happen to sit next to us…

                    (another fateful encounter,
                    fateful women in my life)

They meet before shift for cappuccino—
Margaret I date briefly & years later Mindy
with the ever elusive promise of love,
& finally she comes through…

                    & a novel is born the next table over—
                    But who tells the Story that really needs
                                          telling?

& there's Willy, sly devil, disappearing & reappearing
    every so often
& quiet Sam from Sonoma, his periodic returns
& Craig & Steve, surrealists in real life purgatory
& David on the fringe discovers success with high-tech
& Anna popped into town a season now is off to The City
& Robbie, with a thousand trails of friends in every direction,
    always spontaneous, *Let's go dancing!*
& Mat is sceptical, *Who is this woman?*
    Another Santa Cruz flake?

& Dr. Wolff, numerologist, plots cosmic/social cycles
& Dorothy sits modestly, always collecting her male curios
& old time socialists talk endless politics…

    In the White House
    a new shuffle
    of politicians—
    But the Vision
    to guide us?

The Perg, Diane from Connecticut called it,
driving up the coast from Santa Barbara,
seeking a new life in California—
But where to settle?
    The Cruz?

        to die upon
        to purify

They come, year in & year out—
Endless parade of comings & goings,
endless faces, endless talk,
my red brick archive of memories…

        remembering
        their stories,
        weaving into
        the great Story

          to listen
          to engage
          to sympathize
          to counsel
          to help tell

        woven into Vision
        Seed of futurity

        to purge & prepare

Beguiling time
here
stands still

but the world
we must all reenter

to act

forever & ever

accountable

1989
originally behind the old Bookshop SC, Pacific Ave.

Café Caméléon

Better change
Better learn how to change

           What place is this?
           What times are these?
           Where are we going?

Creatures of The Edge
hanging on
reptile house
feedin' on sandwiches & coffee,
the air is still free

           these are the basics
           this is survival
           this is tomorrow

this is place called metamorphosis,
of multiplying millennial mutants
this is bizarre town

        to become something other
        something different
        something that survives
        perhaps something that eventually thrives

Pushed to The Edge
Western relentless push to devastation
this is ABC all over again

      Age of Disorientation

           these are the outcasts
           these are the disinherited
           these are the unclassifiable

bumming through
this menagerie
this orphanage
this half-way house of hope

we suffer the transition of Ages

                abandoned

                homeless

searching for a homeland

pushed to The Edge

        hanging on

                some slipping

                      some pushed over

& the great arms of Ocean
take back

        we succumb, we die

or, like the chameleon, change...

                          And the funky back room,
its chipped, pocked, white painted cinder block walls,
art works screaming out, light bulb bare, the cheap
painted tables & black painted plywood stage,
is a venue for
                poetry readings, music/multimedia shows,
comedy, plays, skits, & a drawing class of Tuesday night
nudes

   & Michael the pianist plays beautifully,
when occasionally he plays

Mobbed evenings try finding a table—
They serve cakes, cappuccinos,
soup, soda pop, hot spiced cider,
sandwiches, coffee, the air is still free

     What is our common ground?
     What do we value?
     What bonds have we?

this is the raw sound of fabric ripping
these are the graffiti languages scrawled
  across bathroom walls
this is the guttural gesture

What shreds of family? of friends?
What shreds of pop culture? of causes? of career?
What shreds of money? of security? of property?
What shreds of thrills? of drugs? of sex?

   Mere survival?

     Nothing more?

these are the shaven heads
these are the metal heads
these are the borderlands
these are the torn-up talents
  would self-destruct
these are the students
  groping into

   What future?

jaded, rumpled, ragged, thrift-shopped, cross-dressed,
mismatched, leather & spikes & tight black skirts,
cropped hair & long hair & multicolored protean hair,
piercings & rings & reptile vacant looks,
disoriented, drugged out, noddin', driftin', hangin' out,
wastin', waitin', perhaps waitin' for somethin',
    somethin' alive & kickin'

        to jump start

  What future?

        these are the maladjusted
        these are the discontent
        this is the sediment
        this is the fallout
        of wealth

mommy & daddy's casualties
the underbelly of television
the breakfast table barrenness
daily freeway fragmentation
this is the devastation

        now years upon us

Who survives?

For what?

        These
among millions pushed to The Edge,
no choice, but practice, hanging on

    clinging

        to The Edge

Millions will be next,
pushed to The Edge,
all the way from Kansas

    needful the metamorphosis:

to change / learn to
as day & night change
as seasons change
as culture must change

        or die

This is mutant town America

    Who survives?

        What life?

           For what?

Dark Age we live through

        transition to

a new creature to be born,
part-divine, half-formed...

& here is John the anarchist
here is Janice the singer
here is Alice the activist
here is Oman the wanderer

        & here is Devera the unconcerned
        here is Twyla, always loyal
        here is Marissa, still searching

& this is Tom the social redevelopment specialist,
come to sit daily among his young friends.

This is the Caméléon
where two weeks in a once November I hung high
    on The Cruz,
where Lizzy Maroon herself had arrived
straight from the Midwest,
& one early summer day popped in on the Caméléon,
got a job, hung out, prepared herself to change colors,
    she changed colors,
& prepared others, to change colors,
    as best she could
               among
      these creatures

        clinging

  on The Edge

1990
formerly on Front St.

The Happy Hour Gang

—Who do you know in the Gang?
*—Scott brought me. I heard so much
   about "the Gang" I had to check you all out
         for myself.*
—Yeah, we're all single here.

That is, 'cept Danny, who's married, they say—
An open marriage, you know, she's rarely with him.

    8-10-15-20-25 & more of us, depending

       take over the place

—Everyone here single?
—Yeah, you wanna join us?
—We need another table!
   —more chairs!—
—Here come Camille & Vicki,
   Lee Ann chirps happily.

      At the Dream Inn
we improvise a circle,
it's Kayleigh's birthday & more keep comin'
& it keeps growin', this circle of singles,
& other people are wonderin'.

—What is this group?
   strangers always ask.
—The Happy Hour Gang.

     It's Friday, isn't it?

Yes, just about everyone here is single, but there is one
   steady couple—
        Rich & Sylvie,
who occasionally bring his kids.

Oh yes, another somewhat steady couple,
    Scott & Jan,
but—they'll break up soon.

     Is anything long-term...anymore?

At first we hardly knew one another,
or at least I didn't know everyone, except one or two—
    Mat introduced me.
We meet a different place every Friday,
    Palomar/Peachwood/Courtyard/Crow's Nest/
        Hungry Pelican
                on the wharf—

(O the surf & sky are gorgeous through the window;
  speechless, I stare off & witness my Vision...)

—Who are you dating, Ral?
  You met her at happy hour?
  You mean that blonde John brought?
  What's her name—Crystal?

                        And I brought Mindy
                        holding hands
                        earlier that year,
                        but we were friends
                        just then,
                        she wanted to meet
                        new people.

            Someone new
            said Crystal,
            & that was me.

And then:
—*Where do we meet next Friday, Gang?*
—*What about the Holiday Inn?*
—*Dream Inn is more comfy.*
—*No, Severino's! They got the best hors d'oeuvres.*

And then next week:
—*Let's meet at The Catalyst.*
—*Too noisy.*
—*But Dancing Man has an opening*

       just two blocks down, round the corner,
           there'll be plenty of hors d'oeuvres & wine

Every Friday week after week
—*How long has this group been meeting?*
    asked the cocktail waitress.
—*What, over a year & a half now?*
—*The same people, that long?*

        Some come & some go
        & at least two dozen others
        on the fringe / keep in touch
        always providing us with parties.

—*Yeah, more or less the same people.*
—*Your group's been through here before,*
   another waitress.

        getting well-known in town

—*Not a club? Don't work together?*
 Then what is it?

        That's a good question.

Singles out socializing among familiar faces,
a safe group, they say, to be among—
it's the ol' Friday bar gatherin' ritual

—*Your Gang sounds like fun.*

And who are these people?

—Teachers/real estate agents/county workers/nurses/
software engineers/computer graphic designers/high-tech
technicians/couple of seismologists/managers/secretaries/
counselors/a university professor/a carpenter/all quite
    respectable

        & a couple of us oddball artists.

Lookin' for someone new
Some no longer lookin'
Early-mid-thirties & up,
most never married
Singles forever single

        but plenty of photos
document the weeks,
Carol & Mindy & Lee Ann are such bugs for cameras.

But they're still strangers to me,
as I undoubtedly to them,
can't get beyond the chit-chat—

        Kimberly & I
        have a hard time talkin',
        from day one
        when I dared express
        metaphysical views.

        What's new?

        Kristine is changing jobs
        Camille's daughter is visiting
        Scott & Patty broke up
        Danny's buying another house

        & Sylvie, teacher of mythology
        at some college in the South Bay,
        shuns myth talk with a living mythmaker—
        that is, *I am*

                    —keep it light, right?

            but Gene & I
            talk Heidegger on the sly

            & Mat & I
            no longer talk much about art
            —too much friction there—
            but women, yes,
            a topic that's safe.

Where are these people going?

To Sue's party tomorrow
    —*What's the theme?*
    —*Wear green.*
& to Gary's party next Saturday.
Then there's Gene's barbecue coming up
& don't forget the beach party on Sunday
& plans for a camp out
& brunch for Camille's birthday.

    —*Oh, you didn't hear about it?*
    —*Only a select few, is it?*

                        & Halloween parties
                        Christmas parties
                        Lee Ann's Valentine's party
                            (costumes risque
                             & games we play)
                        Leonardo's famous, annual
                            Pirates Party

—*Ral, you havin' a party?*
    Gene asked.
—*Well that's nice of you,*
    Kristine, eyes fluttering.

Invitations I pass out,
with a map to my house.
Bring a friend or two,

         someone new

   perhaps someone to join the Gang

But do they ever pair up?

Yes, Paul is dating someone Trish
Mike is dating someone Linda   (outside the Gang
Greg is dating someone Toni   possibilities
Camille is dating someone Bill   are unlimited)

     & John brings someone new every week

It's all temporary, though, they stay the trend,
   80s style,
the fabric of the world all coming undone.
    —It's difficult to really find someone, you know?
    —She's the second one for Scott this year.
It's the quiet, killing frustration;
here, too, the invisible, subtle, devastation...

        Mindy & I
        were the recent item,
        & demonstratively
        notorious at that.
        But it's over now.
        —*That's too bad,*
          said Kayleigh,
        You two lasted awhile.

   but still the closest of friends

    & Vicki sat
    on some guy's lap
    she just met
    a day or two ago—

    That was fast,
    but it won't last

    & John said to Mat,
    *—See those women
     over there?
     Why don't you
     ask them
     to come on over?*

And after Happy Hour there's...

  —Any openings tonight?
  —Bay Photo?
  —Good, they'll have a whole counter
    of hors d'oeuvres.

        or then it's dinner,
        then dancing

—Let's hit the St. James Club!

    Lee Ann & I
    danced that night—
    What exactly was I looking for?

    Or some split off,
    some call it a night,
    or someone is off on a date,
    rendezvous elsewhere
    —Oh, I'll bring him next week.

So it was The Catalyst that Friday, on the mezzanine we met,
 above the crowd & too-loud music, & then, on to Dancing Man
  (where 2 or 3 of the Gang got tipsy on wine);

stiflin' hot & packed inside, we stood outside, stood against my car,
made our own hot scene, & then, it was on to the Bulkhead Gallery,
another whole scene there windin' down
    (—*You brought your drunk friends to our gallery.*
     They kept leaning against the art!)
& then to Lulu Carpenter's & more drinks, us guys flirtin' again
with someone new who just joined on…& what a waste that was,
but Sara had to wait & sober up, didn't want her goin' out alone
    like that…

Or the evening at the Palomar, on the Mall, the Gang streamed in
& then out again—Mindy snapped pictures, we all posed in turn,
    while people kept wonderin' what the deal—
& next, it was the Catalyst, where we met up with others, & more drinks,
then Tampico 'cross the street, Mexican dinner for 9,
& then Pergolesi for coffee, where I strangely ended up
with all the women, that was before Mindy & I…

—*Who do you know in the Gang?*
—*Dave told me about "the Gang."*
—*Oh, so you two know one another?*

    small town

        getting well-known

—*Everyone here single?*
—*Yeah, you wanna join us?*
—*We need another table!*
    —*more chairs!*—
—*Here come Rich & Sylvie,*
    Lee Ann peeps happily.
 Haven't seen them in awhile.

—*And how is Scott doing these days?*

And the Gang still meets,
    two years on—
And I'm still feelin' a stranger,
I just have'ta find my way
    & move on...

1990

Doctor's Advice

This doctor I'm talkin' with
kind'a young & brash & full of self-pride
    —we're standin' round
the backyard of a summertime hospital party,
eatin' chicken, drinkin' beer,
& all these women are leanin' on every word
    he says—
He says to me,
You refuse to make money.
It's a cop out, can't you see?
Your old artist claim of art
& inspiration coming first
is only laziness, lack of discipline—
Look, what you need is a plan.
Make your money first.
Win your freedom—
and he looks round boyishly
    & grins,
hammerin' the free advice,
Win security, respect & women,
and the women, sure enough, sway
to every word, standin' round.
They know the old score.
What, you like bein' poor?

He knows the damn score,
smiles, *You could be well-off*
& forget these petty worries.
You just hav'ta sacrifice your art
    awhile...

His nurse girlfriend,
blonde & buxom & just right
    in every way,
comes up in her low-cut & winks.

Tempting advice,
tempting women standin' round,
& obviously I see my disadvantage,
    I have to agree.
                      But what?
Change what the wise old sisters
    of destiny
have spun for me?

late 1980s

Now I'm In It

Once, it was not long ago,
when I was still climbing out of my hole,
the local highway overpass was a perch
upon which I watched daily the mad flow
              of the Western river,
its endless flow of oil mad hunger.

    I was slower then,
    still being born

        (my years clouded by Pluto)

Now I'm in it,
now I drive,
as I did
when twenty-five

    —Oh, that was another lifetime ago!

More than that, I've been born again
to lead double & triple lives—
Self-diagnosed a polyphrenic,
the multidimensional New Age man,
I circulate among many,
wearing masks where I go,
wearing masks & who would know?

    (Still today,
     only Psyche knows me!)

        *

    Poet pressed to the lonely work,
    bringing Vision into life,
    yet must live somehow—

Back & forth I weave through town,
up & down the county drive,
Team I sergeant
in a security company
this role I've taken
　　　to survive.

Train & train & supervise,
schedules make out, billing reports,
work my shifts & work more shifts & double shifts,
try to eat & sleep, on the phone night & day—
My pager goes beep sittin' workin' on a manuscript
　　　at the Caméléon.
—*Are you a cop? narc? FBI?*
Endless the troubleshooting when responsible
　　　for up to twenty.

My shift at silicon wafer cookin'
Watkins-Johnson is over,
but still more stops must I make
　　　before I sleep—
Salz Tannery (start up boiler,
once again, someone new to train)
then Community Hospital
(visit with Corporal Donna,
　where she livin' now, her new boyfriend,
　　　& all that)
& talk with Sergeant Jim at the Dream Inn
—& I work there once a week.
(I stand on the roof ten floors up,
　& contemplate 360° The Cruz—
　　　　　　　　on the edge
　　　　　　　　of The Edge!)

　　　I'm at the tannery again & again—

      Poet fires up boiler
    every Sunday at midnight!

Who else to do it?

No end of biweekly schedules, monthly billing reports,
meetings with the Boss, reviewing applications,
& they all want me to write a manual—
   —You're a writer, right?

At our Christmas party, I'm presented with

      Employee of the Year
         award

   A poet?
   Who wants to turn the world upside down?
   (as I've been told)

   O the masks we must wear!

              On the way
to Peachwood/Crow's Nest/Courtyard's
summertime back patio, sittin' round,
drinkin', it's happy hour & the Gang's
   all here—
I hang out with all the singles yuppies,
attend all the barbecues & parties.

—Look, she said,
   I have no underwear on—
She flipped up her skirt,
I'm behind the wheel,
headin' straight for my place.

      And on the way
to somewhere

I'm drivin' the freeway & heavy metal
thrashes on the radio—

...over my head I hear music in the air,
                    I hear music...
    sings King's X

—*You listen to heavy metal?*
No, it's life I listen to, the world all around me.
I listen to talk shows, I tap into Christian stations—
Can't ignore the Armageddon plot of the Medieval mind.

                    I listened in long silence
                        upon the cliffs
                      & saw the corridors I must explore
                      guided by Psyche Divine,
                      among the Gods & Goddesses
                        of our being.

            DJ Heavy Hard
would never guess this New Age bard
was listenin'

            & readin' at the Caméléon,
Jeffrey & I poetry / comedy performin',
our concept shows

        "The Lamp & The Monitor"
guiding others
        "In the Labyrinth"

& practice with Jan, her guitar compositions,
we tape together in Errol's home recording studio,
    up in Ben Lomond,
& jammin' again with Jim & Rin.

—*You hang out at the Caméléon?*
    (meaning the riffraff)

No, it's life I hang out with, my love affair,
with inspirations coming at me daily—

      can't keep up with them all

I hear a Melody constantly changing

I see my life pass before me

             on the freeway

     torn asunder I am

  by Gods of the world—

And who could put me back together again?

    Psyche

       the Thread

             the Golden Thread

     weaving

          & reweaving

      the Dance

   as I must dance...

In my cool blue-striped summer sports jacket
I meet with high-tech security director
& introduce our new officer.

     & John from San Jose
     down on weekends for visits
     —I'm barely up & out of bed—
     we go for long philosophical walks

& long solitude hours on the job
writing & contemplating,
at shift change
talkin' baseball
with Greg—

        In one year acquired my first credit card/
cassette player/answering machine—
    a late bloomer on the material plane.

From such a distance I have had to come!
I was always the Distant One

              circulating like air

      like water

     as the Invisible One

Years ago, did I look too long

          into the Sun?

Torn to pieces for what I saw!

        And daily I watch
        Technos & Psyche
        in contemporary
        struggle
        on the edge
        of The Edge,

        Psyche rising
        into the Air
        over The Cruz—
        It is a Vision
        to last
        a lifetime.

I see the New Age
spread before me,
the lonely work
just begun.

1990

IV

*The Great Santa Cruz
Mountains Earthquake*

a poem chronicle

1989 – 1990

Quake At 5:04

Again, at the recollection,
a shudder registers in this Earthly body,
and sweeps through me a loss like love lost
                              overnight—
I am seized, I choke up, I cannot hold back—
The last nine months have been such a trial for us;
such vulnerability as we came overnight to know
     humbles us.
So much is now gathered in recollection,
more than what those 15 seconds alone
     could gather
when I first stood outside the restaurant
                              after,
and wondered,
               Was it over?

It was only beginning...

                    Tuesday, October 17, 1989,
it was 5:04 pm & the Sun was going down—
Suddenly, for 15 seconds, Earth's tectonic plates slipped
     & shock waves raced—
There was no sign of its coming, no warning whatsoever
     to prepare us,
               the Quake just hit,
the restaurant I sat in walloped
               as if built on a rug,
its edge unexpectedly taken up & shaken—

          kawhoomph! kawhoomph!

Everyone immediately dove under tables;
cups, plates, spoons, knives, forks, glasses jumped
     & clattered & broke,

the floor jumped, all the place jumped,
coffee ran like a muddy torrent all over my table.
We rode the temblor in the shock of those 15 long seconds
& scrambled out after Earth momentarily settled.
The counters were a mess, a window cracked;
but the restaurant held up, we were all still intact.
It was a big one, we all knew,
        the biggest one *we* ever knew—
But where was it centered? the immediate question,
which led to another, *Who took the hit the hardest?*
And quickly we realized
                the power

        was out

The food on my plate, I didn't have the stomach
    to finish;
and the waitresses fluttered about, in a tizzy
    to close up.
Cash register didn't work, meals were on the house.
    I stepped outside,
                the extent of it

        I had no idea

The evening on 41st Avenue in Capitola
    was balmy & clear,
a lilac tranquility hung in the air,
and by chance I saw two friends Chris & Gene
    outside another restaurant,
                          next door—
We talked alarmingly a moment
& then suddenly we were ridin' another,
the parking lot ripplin'

                Earth would not stay still

Gene's car we stood next to, its radio turned on;
but stations winked out, then came back on—

> *...big quake...epicenter near Santa Cruz...*
> *...news helicopters report...*
> *...portion of the Bay Bridge collapsed...*
> *...Nimitz freeway collapsed...*
> *...fire in San Francisco...*

Nothing yet about Santa Cruz—
We didn't know our Pacific Garden Mall
    lay in ruins,
didn't know if any had perished...

        Cars were fleeing fast
the shopping mall nearby,
a free-for-all it seemed at every intersection.
I waited awhile before driving off,
extremely cautious, as if a war had broken out.
Venturing into this evening unforeseen,
    super-alert,
             I kept thinking:

> *Was this it? Was this it?*
> *Was this the Big One?*
> *What to expect*
> *when I got home?*

Back in The Cruz, the neighborhood, my house,
    all still stood,
but when I saw my room in the fading light
—books, papers, tapes had tumbled from shelves—
    I felt I was hit—
        I choked up, tears came to my eyes.
Yet, we were fortunate—we suffered no damage,
    at least of any consequence.
        (Thin cracks like lightning
            ran through our living room wall,
        'bout all.)

But no power, no lights,
                      & day darkened fast,
my two housemates & I huddled around lit candles
& listened to Jak's battery-powered radio:
       ...epicenter 10 miles in the mountains
            southeast of Santa Cruz...
       ...downtown Santa Cruz devastated...
       ...downtown Watsonville devastated...
       ...fires...homes crumbled...thousands injured...
       ...Cypress Street viaduct in Oakland traps motorists...
       ...big San Francisco Marina district fire...
       ...deaths are reported but toll is unknown...

                 perhaps hundreds

Dusk settled quickly & was restless
    with so many questions;
but to Bob & Jak first it meant eat something,
    eat & survive—

       You never knew when
       it would come round
            again

And Santa Cruz remained wrapped in utter darkness
    that night;
throughout that night, aftershocks rattled us—
Like thousands of others, I didn't sleep well;
every 20 minutes, half-hour, my sensitive window
    would wake me,
always seemingly about to shatter across where I lay.
In south county Watsonville, thousands were forced outside
       & slept that night
—& for many nights following—

                    in parks & fields

          *

BIG ONE HITS SANTA CRUZ

DEADLIEST QUAKE SINCE SAN FRANCISCO '06

DOWNTOWN IN RUINS

all the media announced the following day.

Were hundreds killed?

To the radio I listened, a short drive I took,
   —no work to go to that day—
but I was aimless, had no real direction,
so I circled back & decided best to set out
   on foot
       & see everything up close—
I headed to Soquel Avenue; from there,
   headed downtown.
I would see for myself what in 15 seconds
Earth had done to the heart of our city.

And what I saw & what I heard that day...

               Here & there,
streets were cracked, buckled & fissured,
long cracks coursed through sidewalks beneath my feet;
   bridges were damaged & down;
huge auto showcase windows shattered;
   houses jolted off foundations,
& on a neighborhood block close to downtown a handful
had almost immediately caught fire—a gas line had broken;
throughout the Santa Cruz Mountains, reports of fires,
   houses collapsed, roads impassable
       (& for weeks some would go without power, water, gas);
thousands were left homeless, businesses were destroyed;
the main artery into The Cruz—Highway 17—closed by landslides
   (cars dodged boulders when the Quake hit
            —a miracle no one was killed);

& a Highway 1 bridge over a slough outside Watsonville
    also was closed—
               Santa Cruz was nearly isolated;
& we were still without power;
& Aptos Village was also hit,
& tiny Corralitos closest to the epicenter;
& Watsonville, of course, was hit quite hard;
& just over the summit, downtown Los Gatos was also hit hard;
& people were found crushed to death in cars
when, up in the Bay Area, the Oakland overpass collapsed;
& disaster relief started pouring in,
& many in panic grabbed all the supplies they could,
& the San Francisco Bay World Series was postponed until...

              no one knew when

        Yet, there were whole neighborhoods
left undamaged (relatively—some cracks in walls,
              here & there, a chimney tumbled);
& homes perched on hillsides were shaken,
    but amazingly left undamaged.

I walked in the harsh heat of the Sun that day
& saw that our Pacific Garden Mall, the heart center of our city,
had already been closed off, tightly barricaded, police & security
    posted on all corners.
And we, the people, so many of us came to gawk & take in,
          & tried to comprehend,
the beloved heart of our city
we realized
      was gone

Streams of all-age onlookers lined up along the barricades
    & yellow tape,
lots of cameras & camcorders recorded the Quake's aftermath;
in eyes I saw shock & disbelief, teary sadness & long silence—

From the distance allowed us, we saw the collapsed facades,
walls crumbled, roofs caved in, sides of buildings ripped open
    like terrible wounds,
the street, sidewalks & cars under brick & splintered wood,
    splintered were the trees...

        Mortar dust
hung in the air
(& hung for weeks around the Mall)

      This was the heart of our city

Already two dead were pulled out from ruins of what were once businesses
    along the Mall—
A grandmother from under the collapsed ceiling of Ford's Department Store,
& a young man under the collapsed brick wall of the Coffee Roasting Company.
Another woman was uncovered shortly after the Quake from Ford's,
    badly injured   but she pulled through
        —a well-known photo her rescue—;
& many others that day were dazed & injured;
& a vigil was underway for another, a young woman last seen
in the same Coffee Roasting building.
        —Found a day later,
            she was not alive.

        And poured in the national & world media—
        Reporters & TV crews all wanted their visuals,
    & conducted for their audiences on-the-street
      interviews.

And all day we heard,
    How many still trapped beneath the freeway in Oakland?
All day & all night came on the nerve-wracking aftershocks,
& helicopters were flying constantly over us in the skies above,
            & still no power.
Round the clock, local KSCO broadcast emergency info
& Red Cross & disaster volunteers & help & supplies
poured in from around the nation,
            all going into action.

And quake victims were offered refuge in our Civic Auditorium,
& a tent city for thousands had sprung up
    in Watsonville.
        (It was considered the hardest hit of all—
            Whole blocks of Main St. damaged beyond repair,
              & its beloved St. Patrick's Church steeple
                    was badly jolted loose & could not be saved.

And day after day, who didn't hear the question,
    Where were you when it hit?

& day after day all the stories we heard of heroes
    & survivors
& those who veered miraculously from death.

        But 6 *had* died in the county of Santa Cruz,
& stories of hardship of those who lost something of their life
    were the fare of daily papers.

        Officials, of course, poured in—
state, federal, FEMA, the Army Corps of Engineers.
Three days after the Quake, Friday, October 20th,
a big media event was highlighted
           when
President George Bush & Governor Deukmejian
strolled the Mall in an entourage of state & city & county officials,
our mayor Mardi Wormhoudt under tremendous pressure
    & demand
        that things quickly get done.

And entertainment celebrities came through,
offering consolation, promising aid,
& some performing at benefit concerts,

& everyone locally naturally appreciated all the help,
thankful for the heart-felt focus.

        *

So quick our loss before the greater power
    of Earth,
so fragile, isn't it, our little life—
        And it was only a moment's release
    of tectonic tension
        that changed lives forever.
More quakes...still perhaps a bigger one,
   the really Big One,
        perhaps is yet to come...

      After all, *this is earthquake country*

      And that October 17th
        memories of one were conceived

And memories now remind us,
   an era is over—
No more to walk the Mall we once knew
No more the favorite bookstores
No more the café in the courtyard
   (the years I spent there!)
No more the Cooper House
   (a serious blow to local history)
No more all the old buildings
that gave our downtown
the character we all knew
   & loved
No more those who
   met
an untimely death...

      It went down in history
as the Great Santa Cruz Mountains Earthquake of 1989
—or, as you might also hear it referred to,
    the Loma Prieta Quake,
as it struck under the panoramic-seeing eye of our tallest peak.

Seismologists confirmed it was a 7.1
(though some still debate it might have been a 6.9),
    at 11 miles down, under the redwood mountains
        of Nisene Marks State Park, above Aptos
    (go today to the exact spot & you'll find a marker)
& no question, it was the largest quake since San Francisco '06.

Damage in the greater Bay Area is in the billions going up;
but far fewer fatalities occurred than were feared—
                                    67 it stood at
(They say our building codes saved us,
                              & luck—
thousands at the World Series in Candlestick Park
    meant less traffic on the doomed viaduct)
& 14,000 altogether were left homeless;
the ragtag tent city in Watsonville
    maintained itself for weeks.

                                    And for weeks
gawkers would stare through the Mall-encircling fence
    (& I was one)
For weeks the demolition crews went daily to work
For weeks so many stood witness to the old buildings
    coming down
For weeks merchants worried & despaired
    over losses
For weeks the ghost town pall over downtown
For weeks the heated issues with city officials
For weeks the endless earthquake talk
For weeks the news articles & updates
For weeks the changed & new perspectives
For weeks the community pulling together
For weeks jittery nerves jumping
    at every tremor
For weeks the anxiety, flare ups,
    & short tempers
For weeks the grief & tears
For weeks the Quake relief
    & counseling

For weeks the renewal of a spirit
    for rebuilding
For weeks children sharing
    Quake stories in school
For weeks our Town Clock
    still stopped
            at 5:04

And the weeks became months...

        *

The weeks gathered anew
what 15 seconds had shattered.
Now, 9 months later,
recollection's gathering
has given
        birth.

July 15-21, 1990

A Small Victory

for Jeffrey Armstrong

And Jeffrey said,
    Ten years of my life are in that office!
    Has a man no right

              to risk
                          & reclaim his life?

    No,
said the city official,
    No entry will be allowed.

The city official said, because the structural engineers had said,
(who hadn't even gone inside, to see for themselves)
    That building is unsafe for entry.
    It's been red tagged for immediate demolition.

At the Monday meeting of official city pronouncements,
the city official was adamant:
    For the public good, no entry.

              As if people
              hadn't suffered
                  enough—
              What is the public good?
              That more lives be ruined?

And tenants of buildings condemned—50, 60 were present—
sat stunned, in shock, to hear the sentence of their own city
    against them;
with groans, their hearts went down in a swallowing sea
    of no recourse.

In those buildings
whole careers & life works,

entire book & album & art collections
—$150,000 worth of artwork to be lost
      in the Cooper House alone—
years of client files, business records, historic artifacts,
antiques, fine furniture, classic prints, posters, mementos,
photos, all must go, trashed by the rush

       to demolish

  No entry—
said the city official.

Tenants sat stunned, in shock, but not Jeffrey—
He spoke up, questioned, protested,
  I was in that building an hour after the Quake.
  I saw the inside,
      intuition told me
  it was all right up there.

    I saw for myself!
    I was there!

  Sir, our lives remain in those offices.
  Have you no compassion?

It was the same building, in front of, days before,
that President Bush had posed for pictures,
the Hihn's gaping wound spilling out the guts of lives
  for the nation's news-hungry audience.

And Bush reached out & touched it
& all the power of State through his hand flowed:
  That the nation now joining us may know,
  we pronounce this a condemned building.
    So be it.

The same week that space shuttle Atlantis
sent hurling toward Jupiter
    the probe Galileo
Jeffrey stood before the city official,
who had a phalanx of officialdom behind him,
& Jeffrey still insisted,
    But, sir, could you please give us
    some consideration—

And the city official said,
to waylay the voice of protest,
(Jeffrey apparently
  was beginning to stir up the others)
    Okay, we will reevaluate.
    Everyone be back here on Wednesday.

And the mayor knew nothing about it
    —What issue?
when Jeffrey came up to her the next day
    & asked.
The City Planning Department
didn't even know the address—
    What building? The Hihn?

Jeffrey saw the obfuscating sleight-of-hand,
    at work in officialdom,
and on Wednesday morning the window of fate

                  opened

The city official had privately told him,
    I'll tell you right now, you're not going in.
    We haven't changed our evaluation.

And Jeffrey knew, now or never, a man
    must act.

        He saw
        He was there

                (Three people had already died on the Mall,
                        day of the Quake,
                    and the city feared for others.

                        But why the rush

                                to demolish?

            Has a man no right

                        to risk
                                & reclaim his life?

It was now or never—
                    Pacing along the cyclone fence,
looking in at ten years of his life
        —& the lives of others—,
                the heart center of the city
                                cordoned off,
                        No entry—
    Jeffrey knew a man must act.

Closely he watched the guards, waiting for his moment,
        opportunity fashioned by fate & courage—
He grabbed a tree limb overhanging
        & swung himself over
                —he was martial arts practiced—;
it was 7 foot over, & not a sound,
unseen but for one passerby
who felt duty bound to go & tell
while Jeffrey scurried to his building,
& then up the main staircase went;
        once inside,
it was as he had remembered it—
ceiling plaster littered the halls was about all.
Still, his senses remained alert,
        he was no fool—
The Quake had opened up & dropped to the street
a portion of a wall, now but a pile of rubble.

                    To the rear,
in his office, he shut the blinds,
        went to work:
He gathered his things/his life together,
depositing it all at the top of the staircase;
a whole hour he spent up there,
proving what the engineers had failed to
—it was certainly alright up there—,
    he did what he had to do.

                But—
    He *had been seen.*

Two police officers, searching,
        building to building,
                came up the staircase,
        guns drawn;
they heard movement, it was him—
                they zeroed in:
Jeffrey, now caught, put his hands up
                        in surrender,
& said,
    Hello, officers.
    No need to shoot.
    I have an office up here.
    Only gathering my things, not loot.

Naturally they arrested him, crossing a police line,
    for one thing,
                in a disaster zone—
Two pair of handcuffs they slapped on,
    they laid in,
                Why'd you do it?
                You fool—!
speaking to him as if he were a common criminal.

            In the squad car,
Jeffrey turned it around,
advanced his case,

> *Look, I am not a criminal,*
> *I am a citizen.*
> *I respect you, please respect me.*
> *I did what I had to do.*
> *Has a man no right*
>
> >   *to risk*
> > >   *& reclaim his life?*

And one officer he won over:
> He said he would have done it too.

And at the station, as he was booked,
Jeffrey opened up & told his story
& other officers also sympathized:

> > *Why is the city*
> > >   *doing this*
> > > >   *to its people?*

& by one officer he was recognized,
> *Aren't you the high-tech comedian?*
> *I saw you perform once.*

> *Yes, Saint Silicon I am,*

& he offered them a quickie,
> they were aching for a laugh,
> >   & was then released
> on his own recognizance.

> >   The timing was perfect:
Half an hour later,
at the Wednesday meeting, as planned,
where citizens faced city officials,
Jeffrey announced, just as it began,
> *I am proof the building*
> >   *can be entered.*

I was just there for an hour.
I saw for myself.

    & was cheered by all.

But the city official said,
with a lizard-like expressionless face,
  No. No.
  No change.
  No entry.

    Then we will fight it!
those gathered declared, banding together.
The building owner, bold to join in,
the tenants—attorneys among them—,
promised an injunction against the city,
  its shameful rush

      to demolish

  Suspicions surfaced:
  The city wanted hands
  on the FEMA funds,
  had to meet the deadline

  & sacrifice the citizens

The historic Cooper House would go first—
Everything would fall to the wrecking ball,
scarcely a piece of a life would be saved.
The Hihn Building was next—

    But a friend of a tenant,
a structural engineer who was sympathetic,
volunteered to go in

    to see for *himself*—

> *If Jeffrey did it,*
> *then I will*
>   *& take photos*
>   *inside*
> *to present*
>   *to the city*
>   *officials*

    who relented

     *

We gathered
on that good Saturday morning—

  I volunteered to help
     Jeffrey & others
   to risk
    & reclaim
   the pieces of their lives

  Beyond the fence,
the ruined Hihn
  awaited us.
     But formalities were first
in the staging area:
Instructions, waivers of liability signed,
badges issued, hard hats
   —mumbo jumbo & abracadabra—
& the well-guarded gate
to the heart center of the city

     was opened

I drove in, with an official escort,
our battered Pacific Garden Mall to both sides of us,
store fronts boarded up over all the shattered
  windows

—brick facades had come down on some—,
    & doors hung
           crooked in their frames,
everywhere dusty mounds of rubble
& earth moving equipment
    doing
           their dirty work...
It was brutal, to see up close
what had been done
        to the heart
           of our city.

      Only fifteen minutes
were we given,
& our guide was the good engineer.
Jeffrey & a friend worked upstairs
    in the building
& two of us in the street
loaded up the ten years of his life,
& then what we all could
of the lives of others in the building,
all these hard hat officials
    keeping close eye,
one or two lending a hand,
& police & fire department
    stood close by,
& pictures snapped
& reporters from the fence
    asked questions...

           Those watching from the fence
           cheered when we finished.

And all that day Jeffrey went on
to help others elsewhere
to salvage & risk
    & reclaim their lives—
       It was hardly enough time,
       not enough time.

But they all did what they had to do—

For Jeffrey,
a small victory.

Fall 1989

To Build Again

The city will build again,
the *people* will build again.

     But a sad time it has been
& depressing
these last few months
to walk our famed Pacific Garden Mall,
largely reopened—to pedestrians primarily—,
& yet, the reality is there, we cannot deny it—
No longer is it the ol' Mall we once walked
     before.
Unchecked weeds have invaded the vacant,
rubble-strewn, wretched-looking pits
     of basements
interspersed among the buildings still standing
where once we shopped & lounged
     & conducted business.

Those weeks after the Quake
     we watched
a chapter of local history come to a close;
day by day we watched
               the demolition—
One-third of the Mall's buildings
     would come down.
The newer ones survived.

Daily the cranes & wrecking ball
& clam-shell scoops & bulldozers went to work—
The Cooper House fell first
              (resisting the first blows,
as if too proud, bringing tears to some among the many
                  who had come to watch)
& then the Hihn Building & Ford's Department Store
—now a parking lot, you can drive right onto
     the tile floor—

        (Ford's in Watsonville
        also came down—
        was the oldest
        family-owned business
        in the county.)

& CaféZinho (once the ol' Pergolesi)
—will always be the café in the courtyard
    in memory—
& the bookstores & so many more

    all had to come down...

                One afternoon,
I sat with Jak & Jan in the Pontiac Grill
& we watched out the big-walled windows
the Good Times Building reduced to a layered mass
of devastation by the giant insect machinery.
    (& Jak spoke of the Phoenix that would one day rise)

During those weeks & still months later,
those of us who wandered there,
    taking in its atmosphere,
were bluntly confronted with the loss
    & emptiness we all shared.
Full-of-life once, the Mall we saw
was humbled by the encircling
of cold fencing & rows of barricades
& all the ugly gaping holes
    tourists gawked at.

    Wreathes & flowers
hung from fences
for those who died,
for the heart that was hit.
Pavilions erected in the weeks following
    the Quake
               did business—

It was Christmas

Keep Downtown Alive

Shop Downtown Santa Cruz

the city pleaded.

    A tall tree
    decorated
    on Ford's property
    showed the spirit
    of a community.

And the pavilions packed shoppers
  a holiday season,
but then came winter & so few...

     As we walk today
our Mall of memories,
corridors of fencing direct
  our passage—
The pitted lots littered with brick
& foundation concrete, boards & broken glass,
twisted piping & metal, will someday
  —2 years, 5 years, 10 years?—
    raise buildings again.
For now, a few sculptures of plywood
& bright splashed color attempt to cheer up.
A couple blocks of unsafe buildings
yet stand, decisions awaiting.

     You look up,
and there, at the Trust Building's
topmost corner, one lone brick juts out,
held suspended & level in mid-air
by a fraction of an inch
  still wedged.

And that's the way it is—
a fraction of an inch,
fraction of a second,
between falling & not falling,
between crushed & not crushed,
between living & dying.

And this is what we do,
build & build again, our world
made manifest on the skin of Earth.
And this is what Earth does
and has done
numberless times before

        & since—

    40,000 killed in a quake
    in Iran since,
    1,600 killed in the Philippines
    just last week.

Earth is in constant movement,
whether we register it or not,
and so is Spirit in constant movement
    —& far more so—
giving us a will to rebuild.

Greater than us in Her power,
Earth let us respect,
and let the new Vision of Santa Cruz
    emerge
        & embrace
both Earth & Earth's people.

July 1990

V

A Season of Fire

2020-2021

The CZU Lightning Complex Fire

                    Fire started on Sunday,
August 16, 2020, lightning was the culprit—
They say some 11,000 lightning bolts filled the skies
over the Santa Cruz Mountains & Bay Area
    that freakish storm night.
The CZU Fire spread to 86,509 acres
in 38 days, in San Mateo & Santa Cruz counties,
devastating Butano & Big Basin State Parks—
Historic buildings, such as the Visitor Center,
in Big Basin, were burned to the ground.
Thousands were evacuated in San Lorenzo Valley
—was the entire Valley—, all the way
    to Scotts Valley.
1,490 buildings over all were destroyed,
several hundreds of them were homes.
Fire was 100% contained by September 22,
though the upper roots of redwoods,
just under the soil, were still found smoldering,
despite the rains of early winter,
    well into 2021.

2021

The Freak Storm

For some reason I woke up before 3 am—
A totally silent Sunday wee morning hour;
all the night was stilled, hushed in sleep.
Then, was only minutes later, out of nowhere,
with no warning whatsoever,
a tremendous freight train gust of wind swept in,
sounding immediately like a bombshell of rain;
I had never heard such a freakish wind before.
Suddenly Rhonda was at my door, & said,
Come outside. You have to see this.
In moments I readied myself to step outside
& rain it definitely was not, though it sounded like
pounding rain; all that really came down
     were a few drops.
It was a continuously relentless, unbelievable wind
that augured a novel night of total havoc.
Quickly came on the spectacular lightning,
as later we were told, largely hidden from us
     by the ridges & trees...
but the thunder, the thunder, was tremendous;
this was an extremely rare occurrence
     for summer here.
The lightning, attendant thunder, was ominous,
but soon moved north, with the wind fading out.
Still, an hour later, though, we could hear
the tireless sound of thunder
     far in the distance.
                This was all prelude,
as lightning strikes into our forests came down,
came down, prelude to the catastrophe of fire,
beginning the next day...& day after day
     after that...

        In the morning,
debris littered every square inch
of ground—tons of leaves everywhere,
small & large pinecones, branches large
& branches small, twigs & more twigs,
    all manner of detritus…
a carpet of the aftermath of the freak storm
went down every road, all the way into town.
But little did we know what was coming…

morning of August 16, 2020

Falling Ash

                    The fire had started
north of us sometime on Sunday,
already to begin its rampage of destruction
in Butano & Big Basin State Parks—
Through Monday & Tuesday it raged,
raged upon the ridges & into the deep forest
canyons of our mountains, smaller fires merging,
reaching across into Bonny Doon…& now
     it was Wednesday.
We in Felton were still conducting our everyday lives
on Monday & Tuesday, but with an increasingly
uncomfortable sense that disaster hung in the air—
The utterly smoke-filled sky tainted a dull
     yellowish gray;
we could hardly see the distant ridges;
the telltale strong smell of smoke
was inescapable wherever you went.

                    On Wednesday
I was sitting at one of the outside tables
of The White Raven café down in Felton,
as most days I do,
              & black & white,
mostly delicate white, ash kept silently
falling out of the air, flecks of white falling,
falling on my table & computer, as I worked.
There was no one out on the community deck;
there was scarcely anyone about anywhere
on the downtown strip.
                      The café
had already closed early—its new owner Rose
came out & chatted with me at my table about
what was happening ominously all around us.
All the shops along the strip were closed.

Blackened redwood leaves, mixed with ash,
were now starting to fall around us, falling, falling,
right out of the air, a steady falling on the table
    as we sat.
Every business in Felton was closing early.
All of Felton received an evacuation warning that day;
we began to think of what that reality meant.

        Early the next morning
we then received the evacuation order.
That morning our cars were covered in white ash.
And ash kept falling out of the sky as we quickly began
to gather our valuables, clothes, & all manner
of sundry items into our cars.
                      The owner
of our house, however, secretly stayed behind,
to save our house, if it came to that.
The Sun was a solid orange disc popping out of
the dense smoke sky. To look directly at the Sun
    was no hurt to the eyes.

day of August 19, 2020

Our Martian Sky

The very day that fiery Mars in Aries,
the supreme sign of Fire, went retrograde,
we woke up in disbelief to a new sky,
a surreal, otherworldly, Martian sky—
Every direction we turned, every step we took,
our eyes saw our surroundings through an eerie
    orange-red hue.
We were now living in, having to adjust to,
    another world.
Fires still burning from afar had altered
    our atmosphere.

Later, sitting at the café I frequent in Felton,
as the afternoon progressed, the sky became
an even deeper, darker, uniform, monochrome,
    apocalyptic red,
& day fell into a darker & darker premature dusk.
By late mid-afternoon, all cars had lights on.
It was a suspended rust-tinted dusk that would
    drag on for hours.

September 9, 2020

We Now Know...

We now know what it is like to be given
such an order as we were given that morning—
To immediately evacuate because of fire,
as fire was fast coming down the mountains...
to suddenly be uprooted from our daily life—
To have to find shelter for who knew how long,
to be an evacuee, a refugee, in another town.
Now we know what it is like to agonize
about the fate of our house, not knowing
    if it was to be saved or not—
To pine about what we left behind,
what we might never see again.
To wonder where we might eventually
    have to move.
To spend nights rummaging among
dark, depressing imagery of fire ravaging,
    to come so close to loss.
(The fire came to less than a mile of our house.)
Now we know what it is like to be
thankful, in deep gratitude, to the firefighters
    who saved our towns.
Now we know what it is like to hear, however,
the grief & sorrow & sadness of others
    who lost everything—
(Our friend Peter, living just outside
Big Basin, lost everything.)
And what were they all to do?

September 5, 2020

A Snapshot as I Sit

Sitting on a bench in our new
little pathway Felton Discovery Park,
I am gazing at the Sun, two weeks of smoke
    has largely dissipated—
An enormously destructive fire is still raging
in the Santa Cruz Mountains north of us though,
a fire that had threatened our town of Felton
& the entire San Lorenzo Valley;
our town was, with deep gratitude, saved,
as were the other towns in our valley;
Felton has now been slowly returning
to the former life we all loved here.
Everywhere in town are signs that read,
Thank You Firefighters! Thank You First Responders!
    Felton Loves You!
Behind me some minutes ago, a dozen police
vehicles & unmarked black government limousines
had a whole block closed off—publicly unannounced,
in secrecy, our governor Newsom had made a personal
    visit to Felton.
Sheriff vehicles daily patrol the streets constantly.
Back on the community deck, we heard stories
of evacuation, of homes lost—in the several hundreds—,
such anguish, emptiness of despair, such sadness,
    we heard,
& of homes fatefully, even miraculously, saved,
& what areas of the valley had now been reopened.
A couple caught up in an emotional scene in a truck
had parked right beside where I had parked
    back at the deck.
People wearing masks go into our favorite, local
Wild Roots Market, which reopened yesterday.
A small friendly dog—a corgi—appears out of nowhere
& almost jumps on my lap, starting to lick me.

Its owner suddenly appears—a long leash she holds—
& says, "Sorry," then, "She likes you."
A helicopter comes & goes over the near ridge,
is now circling overhead, surveilling the terrain.

      I am sitting on a bench relaxed,
contemplating it all & all we went through,
a full 9 days to evacuate at a friend's place
    south of Aptos.
A black phoebe alights on a post near me
& we peer at & commune with one another
    for a good few minutes.
This is the brightest I had seen the Sun
in over two weeks.

September 1, 2020

VI

Happy Hour: The Catalyst

Other nightclubs have come & gone,
The Catalyst is forever...

It's Happy Hour Friday Catalyst style,
   like, goin' way back,
       this packed lettin' all the weeklong pent-up talk
         break out,
     with music hittin' ya head-on like a loud Mack truck,
all comin' & blastin' atch'ya
        the moment you walk in—
You've entered the Garden Room
& Wally's Swing World all dressed in clean cut black & white
is puttin' out a whopper of sound the floor is jumpin',
        whirls of swing dance couples are doin' it right—
After all these years
Wally's Swing is still performin' as if only last Friday I were here
                —it's been years—,
   —& years further back of that
            the Dixieland Abalone Stompers
were puttin' out the weekly Happy Hour blast—

        & how the world the world the world
     spins on & on,
  & the couples still swing to it,
     they've got the number of this place,
              they really dig it,
     such a groove so easy to slip into,
the big bomb of echo in the bright bright air,
   the slant ceiling of lattice beams translucent,
     all open feelin',
        pourin' in all this light
—a windowed wall facin' the street its glass shutters
    thrown open—
       it's all another kind'a cathedral-like,
         showered in light—

& it hits ya, this plant lavish place,
        vibrant green the eye sees everywhere—
big ferns hangin' from the beams & forest leaf splendor
      spread overhead
              & large planter box big-leafed tropicals
   with their spindly branches,
                    & barroom fans are twirlin',
a big rowboat hangs above all the action,
plenty of people-congregatin' at solid wood-topped tables,
       & some of the old Gang I see are still here,
   it's been like years
      —like 10 years—,
          we'd meet & yak & head off
to parties & openings & points here & there
   & in between...

& the crowd spills over to the back wrap-around bar,
   a green leather sofa some guys & gals
     are yappin' on nearby,
& to the further back big performance room
               —the concert is later—
   others scatter to dim & quiet,
but here,
     at the back Garden Room bar & at the tables,
       in the aisles & on the dance floor—
yap yappin' the mouths are goin' & drinkin,'
    it's a mad happy roilin' clamorin' scene,

& local artist dance extraordinaire Ed Teitcher
  is hot dancin' with an equally masterful
    long-legged beauty
in the main front
    —get-out-of-their-way—
                  food counter aisle
where the bright color quirky murals are,
   they're dancin' like they're oblivious to others,
like stars they think, actin' in their own fast movie,

                 & then the music stops, like, this is it,
        & the dancers clap for an encore number
             & so Wally & gang
     hit it again
        with all they got
                 & the couples swing & jitter & twirl
like this is really it now till next week,
                      better do it—

       & suddenly the music the music the music
  is over
          & a roomful of voices sends up huge
   a reverberating echo
& then goes the loud clang of the bell for last call,
       better get yourself up to the bar quick—
   And so another Happy Hour
  closes
     at The Catalyst,
   another weekly slice of Wally's swing pie,
     like, served up—

And over the entrance of this scene,
there is a figurine of what must be
   yes, *Jesus*,
encased in a plastic display box,
with a pink neon halo,
caught in the pose
of strummin'
a guitar...

1011 Pacific Ave, Santa Cruz
July 1999

Pontiac Grill: Memory Corridor

Like, really Fifties nostalgia this joint,
how it takes me down this memory corridor,
that time when Viv & I once sat here eye-to-eye
in one of these red vinyl white trim booths,
the night world lost in lights outside the wrap-around wall-size
    self-reflecting windows,
hot neon red running along top,
upside-down white cones of light hangin' over,
50s style soda fountain counters,
& red padded counter stools,
&, as in the old days, ketchup & mustard squeeze bottles
    sittin' on all the tables...

        Our local drug store back when had a soda fountain,
          I'd pull up on my bike with Mom's
              tranquilizer prescription—

        & a waitress handed us red menus,
          the grill of a Pontiac grinnin' at us

            Find your thrill at the
                Pontiac
                Grill

We flipped open to
    burgers & fries, mash potatoes & gravy meatloaf,
    ice cream sundaes, we wanted a shake—

In those days when the promise of new romance
began to flower,
        like, once again,
we sat there,
trying to recapture that Fifties thing,
these small carousel-style juke boxes at each booth,
we're catchin' *Elvis* croon...

And I remember my dear Aunt Terry
    playin' her Elvis records
        on a torrid of a summer afternoon;
          young & still single,
            she lived with sis, Aunt Peggy,
              at our grandparent's house,
the simmering, waiting, stay-at-home Virgo—

Oh, I just remember—
        Viv was a Virgo.

And there's a real grill of a Pontiac
        mounted above the big order counter window
          framed by

      Pontiac   Grill

in warm & desirous orange & lavender neon,
& all this Pontiac memorabilia they got framed on back walls...

    Our family, though—
        No Pontiacs for us,
           always Oldsmobiles for my Dad.
'Bout every summer Sunday after church
      —church, for Mom & us kids—,
we went on family picnics to the beach,
usually little known then Teeple Lake,
           north of Detroit—
    Every Sunday, no matter where,
we went somewhere,
              in our Olds.

So we shared an old-fashioned milkshake—chocolate—,
two straws in a fountain glass
            tête-à-tête

    & compared natal charts,
with what astro makeup we entered this world,
& how we matched up—
              Cancer in common/Libra in common
                              —There's a connection.

And we shared these childhood Fifties/early Sixties memories—

        My family livin' out the American made-for tragedy
                in suburbs westside the Motor City,
            whereas Viv lived here, in The Cruz,
                had seen a lotta changes...

& one after another they're playin' the rotation—
        Roy Orbison
            Jan & Dean
                The Lettermen
                  Chuck Berry
                  Ray Charles
                  Buddy Holly
                    The Crystals
                        Bill Haley & the Comets
                  Patsy Cline
                Doris Day
              Nat "King" Cole
            James Brown
          The Shangra-Las
        Petula Clark
        The Temptations
California's own *Beach Boys*
& of course once again
              Elvis

    And I remember wedding receptions
                    on these sultry summer nights,
  wild Polish polka dancing & drinking till past midnight,
  us kids got so tired, fallin' asleep, hearin' voices & music
                              in our sleep—

    & within a year Viv & I would announce our big plans—
        First time for me, second time for her

        ...and then he kissed me...
                      The Crystals sang
  & that is how
        it should have been,
but apparently
            was not meant to be—

    Always seems here like summer again.

That was the early Nineties,
the Fabric of our world slowly coming undone—
I suppose it was never quite possible again
to recapture that Fifties thing,

& so our future together came undone
long before the vows *I do.*

                Again, here I am,
havin' a shake—chocolate, of course—,
goin' down an ol' memory corridor
            as ol' numbers play

      once again

429 Front St, Santa Cruz
1999

Opening Day Saturn Cafe

The Cruz been waitin' awhile for this—
Been a long time comin' since fire at the old location
   on Mission
                      shut down the old Saturn.
  There's a new Saturn now;
in the weeks before opening, the town
                  was like gettin' impatient,
waitin' & wonderin' 'bout the latest word;
a sign on the door kept promisin'
                    Soon! Not much longer!

           And as chance would have it
    —I really didn't plan it—
I find myself here, on their first full day open,
& it's a whole new look, a new building, a new location
—it's at the far south end of Pacific Ave downtown—,
            & it's already gettin' late—
—'bout 5 hours earlier the doors were thrown open—
& it's certainly an impact, it has,
        how it's all one big circular
              —it kind'a hits ya like that—*visual*.
I walk 'round the outer black Saturn partition ring,
—tables spaced inside & mobiles hangin' everywhere—,
  & tables ring the outer window-walled rim,
     neon stars of various color ring the upper windows—
& every table, of course, been taken,
it's a swarm, voices throng, music loud & poundin',
people are all queued up at the waitin' spot.
            It's a crazy thing they got,
it's sort'a bizarre really—
              a retro diner feel
   where young concept artists were given free rein
      to go, like, very creative wild.

Above a thatched roof overhang
                        over one wall of tables
    a big red heart you see, a banner
            TRUE LOVE
                        wrapped around it,
        pink flowers peekin' out behind,
swimsuit-clad love girls sittin' on either side,
    big red cherries under their arched legs—
                                    Such
    an anachronistic romantic icon throwback
in the actual of our Postmodern decadent jaded milieu.

And in one silvery shiny rainbow corner
                next to the passageway to the kitchen,
there's a sticker photo booth & juke box,
                        a miniature disco ball
            twirlin' overhead,
                        & still—
It's after midnight, place is hoppin' goin' nonstop,
    waiters & waitresses are still workin' in a whirl,
        the whole place is pushed
            —everything-in-motion—
                            to the max.

—Oh, I took a seat at the counter pretty quick
    & already got talkin' with everyone around me—
        & I watch this one mobile, a saucer,
    its rim, how it flashes all this iridescence...
        Seems that artsy flourishes touch everything—
Oh yeah,
        the tables are a trip,
    each one a unique glass-topped display
        of miniature art assemblages, montages,
            clever little crazy scenarios
                down thru the glass
        as you eat,

     —&, by the way, I discovered
  —I got up & walked around—
     if you enter the door at the rear,
  you walk thru a black light of a hallway
      with spacey bizarre art there on the walls,
 & it's really silly bizarre
    the walls
      outside the restrooms
        labelled Rockets & Rockettes—
The artists must'a had a blast.

It's still packed, it's after one...

145 Laurel, Santa Cruz
September 1999

Al Dente: The Experience

It's for the sheer experience
  of it—

You better like it loud, 'cause it's loud in here,
    it's like decibel extreme,
like everyone this neighborhood of Seabright knows the place,
whether it's Rolling Stones, Beatles, or Bee Gees,
    funk, rap, or techno,
a disco ball is spinnin' in the middle of the ceilin'
    like this is some club for dancin',
                        but *it's not—*
            Or, let's say, it's a different kind'a dancin',
it's, like, the whole dance you're part of dinin' here—

                        Lucio Fanni
right there 'cross the counter in the open to all
is workin' the grill, he's jumpin', boppin', hoppin',
    he's like twirlin', he's enthusin',
he's doin' the break dance arm pumpin' action—
    It's a hot pan of pasta
                he's got swirlin' round & round
        like the little spots
                    swirlin' round & round
                            the walls & floor—
A slight, wiry, Einstein-lookin'
    —the bushy silver hair is obvious—
                genius of Italian cookin'
        is in his glory,
    has all the burners of the grill goin' at once,
he's cookin' it all himself, every order, every dish from scratch,
it's the whole experience why this place gets so popular packed—
People think nothing of waiting outside an hour to get in
            —better make an evening of it—,
sittin' with wine & munchin' franchese,

grabbin' menus from a black mailbox at the front window,
stools they've got set out there
    for those waitin' or wanna watch
        Lucio's ongoing hyperkinetic inspiration
          in action,
& waiters & waitresses are, like, doin' the best they can
    to keep up,
      it's a-hoppin',
          it's hip hop time—

There're framed photos all over the walls,
big red motorcycle photo over the back end serving bar station
    where the wine glasses are hangin',
& of course the big framed photo of Einstein
—the famous one with his tongue stickin' out—,
& there's an Einstein puppet too,
          hangin' in the back,
    & Lucio the super-charged, constant movin' dynamo
is sip sippin' the wine & beautifully plyin' up the pasta,
    lettin' the burners, like, all flare up—
      flames leap & lick all over
        the pan he's holdin',
          they're even leapin' inside—
He's singin' & shoutin', barkin' out what dishes are ready,
& the waiters & waitresses are like a dance themselves,
    it's all loud,
      it's spinnin' lights,
        it's nonstop action,
          it's dining entertainment,
& with everyone tryin' the best to talk, it's like a
    Let's shout-above-the-music kind'a party,
      & believe it or not,
        often it gets louder the later it gets.

          And patrons
come up after & pay homage—
Lucio hugs & kisses the women, shakes hands & fakes a kiss
    for the men,

  he's kissin' a woman a second & third time now
    & turns & exclaims, *Now I can cook!*
         & next thing you know
  he's playin' with the light switch
           in beat
     with the low bass
            hip hop
        rhythm—
And intermittently managing to break away,
  he mingles with his equally enthusin' patrons,
    fast Italiano talkin'.
He's dressed in white, white-aproned, white jeans,
  white running shoes,
& you'll also see him holdin' & kissin' babies when families
  pop in to say Hello.
Now for a moment he's standin' at the counter
  —there's a couple there eatin'—,
    he's tellin' 'em jokes & laughin',
  he even does pantomime—

         Lucio,
conductor & master of the Al Dente experience,
  in total command in the swirl of it all—
The huge, deep white round plates keep bein' served up
with delicious—all kinds'a flavors packed—
  perfecta tastin' dishes

415 Seabright, Santa Cruz
August 2000

The Ugly Mug: The Ultimate Café

The name kind'a gets ya, right?
But go ahead, be surprised, open the windowed
double doors & step in & feel how it feels.
If you want a place to kick back, hang out, do your thing,
this is the place, this is the Café of cafés, the ultimate café—
To me—I'm sure to all the regulars—, it's the most comfortable, casual,
friendly, accommodating, be who you are, zone out, get lost in a book,
    study, or leisurely converse for hours, café—
Oh, it's the perfect of rendezvous cafés.

I've always needed a place like this like a second home,
so this, these last few years, is the place I've come to call
    my "second home."
Has the perfect wrap round, espresso, little displays of stuff, counter,
& glass displays cafeteria-style of eats & sweets & that delicious gelato,
& of course all kinds'a espresso drinks, teas & chai, serve yourself coffee
    in big dispensers to the back,
& a whole slew of ugly mugs to choose from alright.
Art exhibited regularly along the long, deep-burgundy-painted wall
where the one, long, continuous bench borders along perfectly sized,
    dark wood tables,
& there're more tables spaced about with solid comfy wood chairs,
& there's even a couple of old-fashioned high-backs to sink into;
there's overhead track lighting, little barrels of light that dangle
over the bench side tables, these ceiling fans circulatin'—
There're usually always tables, or at least one table, available,
'cept on certain school nights it's student packed,
—there're student regulars show up every night—
or on rainy winter weekend afternoons it's like the cozy full house
    place to be
                —if you can find a table then;
but they've also got stools at the big curved window counter
lookin' out the corner of main intersection Porter & Soquel;

& this last year a couple sofas were put in where the big fish tanks
were just earlier put in, one perpendicular to the drift
    of the place like a partition;
& there's a couple hangin' ivy plants spreadin' out overhead,
& down a narrow bulletin board hallway the tiny back restroom
has the very narrow door, white with blue trim inside,
a porthole window flips open,
                      it's like
                            you're on a ship.

Yeah, been hangin' out here goin' on over 4 years now
—it's probably been since '97—place got established in '96—
    & they've all known me here—
                      Colin, Paul, Jason & Aaron,
Boaz, Murielle, Madeline, Maggy & Mandy,
Amber, Niko, Danielle, Carina, Kelsey, Carrie & Kelly,
Rose, Rosie & Rebecca, Jasmine, Jennifer, Melissa, Mike
    & Sean,
& the new Aaron with the little pigtails hangin' down
    behind his ears
(so many of 'em naturally have moved on
        —as we all sooner or later move on—)
& owners Steve & Liz, of course, had the vision
to make it happen,
        they all make it happen,
                this place—

                Almost every evening
after work I'm here, how a life can get to be over time
    conducted here—
How lives unexpectedly intersect, how a place like this can foster that—
One season I led weekly New Age discussions at my table;
    & all kinds'a other groups meet here—
The Sunday afternoon Christian study group guys meet,
various classes meet, & the first Industrial Hemp Expo committee,
my boss director, met here, Jeffrey the Hemp Poet had an office
    'cross the street;

I've met students of Hegel & Heidegger here;
& dates come in for late dessert, there's the leather & tatooed,
    punker-style youth,
& yes, it's also a family kind'a place for some
              —kids, ya know, love gelato—,
& it's whatever gender-oriented friendly;
& traveling singer/songwriter guitarists come through;
they've hosted poetry slams a couple years back;
& Carina of the loud laugh, a compulsive & convulsive jokester
    —you've never seen such spanky energy—,
                      walks in
& there's a round of applause from all standing at the counter,
    —*Okay*—,
       with everybody in the place wondering what the hey,
her voice is poppin', & yeah, she does the loud laugh thing.
And quirkiest & most unpredictable of dress of all,
like, it's the whole whammy of how she presents persona—
    is Rose
        —wouldn't guess it by the name—,
          & Kelsey, too, is most playful that way,
                oh, Rosie, too, so playful at that
   —Rose & Rosie or some combo
        with Kelsey or Carina workin' nights together
          & you've got yourself a guaranteed seat
              for the wackiest time ahead—

        And music, of course, of all genres,
you never know what they'll be playin'—
old disco hits, the 80s sound, Jimi Hendrix or James Brown,
classical, jazz or Gypsy Kings, techno rock or country western,
Pink Floyd or reggae, say, they even get to playin' old Disney movie
    sound tracks.
It's all, you might say, a whole lotta contemporary, multicultural
    diversity
          they got goin' on…

There've been summer days I've been the only one here
—I kept the place alive (as it's been said)—,
             & that's
    how we establish
                       a presence,
  how we all help weave
     just
         by being here,
               by being
     just who-we-are,
the threads of place,
               the poet but another who shows up,
  who articulates—possibly—
    the scene—

              My usual drink
        happens to be
                  the ol' Mug Shot—

Many call it simply *The Mug*.
—As you can see, it's actually quite an attractive mug.

4640 Soquel Dr, Soquel
June 2001

Ciao Bella: Restaurant Eccentric

You ain't seen nothin' like this—

You just know this place is poppin',
the tight, little parking lot like packed, people standin' round,
if you got no reservation, you sure gotta wait—
But the place is so much more than just happens to be popular,
oh, way more, anyone who's been here knows what I'm talkin'—
It's the kind'a place you've always heard these rumors about.
Whether you've ever seen a restaurant
    —you've certainly figured it's Italian by the name—
        decked out like this,
                        I kind'a doubt.
This, like, mad-happy taking-it-to-the-limit, this idiosyncratic,
this, oh, so eccentric, juxtaposed & superimposed Postmodern eclectic—
It's an overload explosion of visual, like, get prepared.
So, if you wanna take a poet's whirl & get a sense of the place,
    here it comes—
                        Just lookin' at the place
from the outside, all decorated like some crazy fairytale fantasy
—was an old funky wood house originally that's next
    the little windy Highway 9 that comes through here—,
           you can see somethin' bizarre's goin' on—
Like the urban wall expressionistic faces painted on the tall wood fence
    on the side,
the flags draped, lights strung up the roof & goin' just about everywhere,
    the gonna-be-late gonna-be-late famous rabbit
runnin' on the waiting deck rail, old 50s-somethin' car seats there
& a gold-painted, naked neutered, like Mad comic andro starin'
    zombie-like at'cha,
& a lovely mademoiselle painted there on the waiting deck wood wall
kind'a naked herself but for grape bunches hung in the appropriate places,
    & a couple other cuties peekin' from both sides,
& then there's something lookin' like an Alice in Wonderland walkway
    goes to the right,
                but we'll take that stroll later…

What greets you is half a manikin in shorts cut off at the waist
to serve as a mini-table for the register book, toothpicks & hard candies
    & a wine glass of flowers—
You step up steps painted purple, yellow, red, green, blue, white, pink,
this well-worn Open sign in the middle with a theatre cordon going up,
the wide opened red doors displayed with old vinyl records,
    album covers & tinsel.

                Oh, it's definitely another realm inside,
like the two red movie theatre seats just inside the door
    suggest—
                      It's the close-packed bar you first walk into,
with tiled counter, cushioned bar stools, beer bottles displayed
    & all your drinkin' establishment kind'a stuff,
but what sure hits you immediately upon first walkin' in, it's the intense,
imploding impact of every square inch of wall in such a space this tight
    all, like, big-time plastered with images—
All manner of celebrity, entertainment, 20th Century icon memorabilia
    is here—
           photos, posters, postcards, comics, decals, collages,
album covers galore, newspaper front pages laminated,
    cut out magazine pictures,
you see neon beer signs, drawings, masks, trinkets, little animals
hangin' down, mobiles, flying dolls, the white ceiling all covered
    with the big round vinyl of records;
        the stars of yesteryear, so many are here—
from Judy Garland, Patsy Cline, Paul Anka, Bobby Rydell,
    —there's Betty Boop I see—,
           Liberace, Sinatra, Elvis, Marilyn, presidential star JFK,
                to Beatles & Cream & don't miss the Mad Hatter hat,
or the Tin Man over the bathroom door, like, you know,
    from the Wizard of Oz.
And over the door you just walked in, there's a shelf of old binders
& photo albums, like, strangely, as if out of someone's attic.
Where I'm sittin' now at this little one-person counter
    lookin' at the menu
        —I got this single seat like pretty quick—

there're books draped across a bungee cord in this sort'a window frame
    that looks out into the central, main room,
        directly in my face a Marilyn Monroe picture book;
on the checkerboard pattern counter, a hand-crafted wooden Buddha,
& there're all these floppy animals around, like this frog hangin'
    on the doorframe next to me.
Through this sort'a window view, the main room you look into
    —it's nothing big, mind you—
has a blue-green marine ceiling, a stylized cityscape wall
    painted with wavy buildings,
        & at the far end behind three poles
there's a narrow silvery-shiny-reflective, with pictured music personalities,
    runway stage—
        Like, what is it they do here now?
Like, I was still in for a surprise, should'a checked out my placemat first,
a photomontage of the routines I see they have been doing recently—
I see it gets risqué outrageous at times.

        As you walk through, room to room,
it all keeps hitting you, this small, closed-in, motley world all its own,
every wall covered with paintings, signs, icons, masks,
everywhere big Alice in Wonderland cutouts;
hangin' down everywhere all kinds'a drapery, bead work curtains,
the side room painted black with colored stars & words shoutin' down
    from the ceilin';
        there's a black light there
along the top edge where all these license plates are displayed
    on one of the end walls,
sparkly crystal balls hangin' down here & there,
        & then the most delightful discovery of all—
The seating outside is arranged right beneath the most perfect
    you could imagine for it of a redwood cathedral,
a dozen or so tall, slender, straight as could be, redwood trunks
    surround the tables,
        going up & up, higher & higher,
this canopy of their branches high above, high up like a sort'a ceiling,
& a disco ball is hangin' between two trunks, there're heat lamps
    & also spotlights mounted.

                              This is where
Rhonda & I, our literally back-to-back birthdays,
we celebrated by a dinner here 'bout 3 years ago October;
friends Denni & Ray joined us, to make a cozy four—
We had a good time, I remember, dining leisurely
     right under these redwoods.
And I see this place has been changin' since that time,
I see it's somewhat the same, but then not really quite the same,
     since that time—
The whole stage thing, I know, was not here before.

                         As I'm indulging now
in this most delicious dish of chicken fettuccini,
dippin' perfect bread in diced up garlic-heaped olive oil
       —it sure is strong—,
all of a sudden three of the waitresses all dressed in black file up
to that narrow—now the spotlights are on—little runway stage
& start dancin' in sync to a long play song,
       like out of the old disco days—
                         "Do Your Thing" goes loud
& everyone, every table, is now turned & utterly riveted on them—
     Yeah, like do it! do it! Do your thing!
And they're good, they're really good, they're dancin' up a sweat.
And so they do this one, long, tremendously upbeat, bursting
       like all out song
           —everyone's into it, like, into it, into it—,
                 & then it's over & everyone claps,
& the next thing you know the three dancers
     are back waitin' their tables.
Other nights when the young owner is around,
I see he puts on somethin' of an erotic pole dancing routine himself,
     as my placemat sure makes quite explicit.
           (but there's another time for more of that—

                              And now
I take the stroll goin' round the Alice in Wonderland
wooden walkway painted with names inside stars,
     like the Hollywood Stars

　　　　　—the first name you see is "Tad,"
　　　　　　　　who happens to be the owner.
And a bench is painted with Tip Toe Thru The Tulips,
there's some big, cutout, cartoony character,
a fish pond, with rocks of blue & pink, & a fountain pourin' out
　　　the rear end of a big fish
　　　　　　　　atop a pseudo-Greek statue;
& little red devils are hangin' about in the surrounding ornamental trees,
& kitschy garden flamingos you also spot, as if stalking about.
　　　There's a sign in red:
　　　　　　　　Men Working.
A beer logo umbrella shades a long, raw wood bench,
& as you walk, more impressions of large & little signs, baskets,
other benches, chairs, big old icon soda pop caps, varieties
　　　of flowers,
& all these words keep grabbin' at your attention, like, nonstop—
　　　　　From one of the redwood trunks facing Highway 9
their own "Ciao Bella" sign hangs,
& there're paintings on plywood, road signs, an Uncle Sam
　　　I Want You U.S. Army poster,
there're bicycle frames, a dog house, one sign-painted board
　　　that says:
　　　　　　We Were Born This Way.
And there's another sums it up quite succinctly:
　　　This Place Is Crazy.

But, you know, I dig this place.

9217 Highway 9, Ben Lomond
July 2002

India Joze: Joe's Own Style

In the front, center pane window
in bright yellow neon, a sign—
Simple:

    ASIAN CUISINE

& big Asian decor stars hang,
in both side panes.
You see people inside sittin' at tables.

Out on the sidewalk a row of potted bamboo,
a couple tables, a small sandwich sign *India Joze,*
easily overlooked—
                  Well, then?
                      Walk in—

                          But what?
Oh, to the left—it's—this? This tiny place?
This cubbyhole of a space? Asian cuisine?
But you're going to find it's a so special place.
Yes, it's alongside this walkthrough to back Studio 418
& its popular dance & performance nights—
Yes, on weekend evenings, especially on the 418 evenings,
this place gets swamped, a line at the order counter
clogs up the whole corridor, people standin' all around
waitin' for tables, waitin' on orders, more people
comin' in, linin' up, standin' round…
(back in the 80s, little does anyone know,
this was location of once Café Caméléon)

                              You see
a motley assortment of artsy colored glass lamps
hangin' down long wires from the high ceiling;
& lights—it happens to be Christmas season too—
    are strung about…

   & three—each different—India Joze signs
are mounted on the yellow walls, above the art works...
It's only got three tall wood tables, one bench table,
one small round table, & yes, a couple of tables
out in the open of the walkthrough there,
& a short, 3-person bar the three of us sit at
faces a seriously splattered window,
with gold & purple stars hangin' down,
that looks straight on into the kitchen...
        And yes, that is Joe there,
dark figure behind the glass, cooking, prepping,
dishing out savory, distinctively original creations...
     Yes, just the other side the window
 he's serving it up—

      Standing at the order counter,
you can also look right on into the kitchen,
a hot, steaming, tight-packed kitchen,
a couple of assistants working the other side
of Joe's magic table...
       And Joe is
constantly in motion
—there goes another splash on the glass—,
& for just a moment he's lookin' down intently...
& the next moment, he'll be steppin' out with a dish—
In round rim glasses, dressed in his uniform chef black—
Spattered black leather vest, dark shirt, black leather hat,
black straps front & back, big metal clip
 on a wide black leather
       utility belt—
  Various prep implements
      swing at his waist
 as he quickly turns this way
      & that—
A big holed cleaver case, a leather holder, a mallet,
long metal spoons, a fire starter, a knife sharpener
on a big metal clip lookin' like a slender
 mini-sword...

He's back in the kitchen intensely focused,
doing magic over the next dish…

        This heaping spoonful of food
    he's dishing up on a plate
            & now here it comes—
       sure is a plateful—
handed over,
        the waitress is comin' through—
zeroes in on
           your table—

       Joe is preeminently
the master artist here,
years of experience he's had creating
these personally designed, complex flavored,
primarily Indian inspired dishes…& exquisite
    Indian condiments besides—
How delicious all these subtle tastes he packs in,
each bite you find yourself surprised at more—
And there's Persian baklava too.

            In the center pane window,
facing in, a block lettered sign, outlined in red:

    May All
    Be Fed

          And yes,
for those who have followed him
through the years, years ago he was
India Joze at the Santa Cruz Art Center—
He was an artist among artists.

418 Front St, Santa Cruz
December 30, 2016

Kianti's Fridays

If you wanna see it,
you gotta time it—

Oh, yes, it must be Friday evening…& it's 7 pm,
    but not always 7 pm—
Look—you know it's happenin' though when
the lights go flashing & the dancing staff has lined up
    & here they come parading out—
It's a packed, full house of customers,
& people are suddenly standing at the door—
Lot'sa pizza & pasta eatin' goin' on, & lot'sa eyes watchin'—
(All the outside tables too are packed this mild June
  of an evening. With the big tall windows, those outside
  also know what's about to break out inside.)
It's their traditional Friday put on a show
    highlight routine—

        The Kianti staff
—there must be ten of 'em—
start to circle about the central partition in the place,
with arms raised, arms now swaying to the music,
pumped up, jubilant, the place is rockin', the music
    is amped,
it's *Celebrate…Celebrate Good Times*,
            Kool & The Gang their song
    their playin'—

        And three of the guys now
raise into the air big rounds of pizza dough—
It's the pizza spinners going to dazzle you alright,
tossin' it up, twirlin' & spinnin' that dough—
Almost unbelievable how they can spin that dough—
Tossing & gyrating & juggling & spinning those rounds
    like tops,

    they spin & spin 'em all around
& catch 'em on fingertips, ah so perfectly
in the center…to spin & spin again,
all eyes are focused on, such a marvel
of good time pizza performance…

     And yellow feather boas
have come out, the circling staff waves them
with arms outstretched, with hands held high,
boas back & forth overhead, yellow streaking,
snapping, in the air, catching the eyes watching,
as the spinners catch the eyes, watching—
The lights are flashing, they go round,
  they go round…
It's *celebrate*—
Everyone's feelin' the good times…

Kianti's Pizza & Pasta Bar
1100 Pacific Ave, Santa Cruz
June 2018

Norma Jean's Coffee: The Name

Now, how could I forget Norma Jean's?
Of course I'll get a coffee, probably a sandwich
—oh, I remember Norma Jean's sandwiches alright—
& perhaps...oh, I'll look over the sweets
when I get there, there're always plenty of sweets
to choose from at Norma Jean's...

        So I walk in
—it's been a few months now—
& it's all so many, so many years familiar—
Just about every day, every weekday morning before work,
& weekend afternoons, yes, about 15 years I was coming here,
both before & after Cathy acquired the old Trout Gulch Coffee
back in April 2005 & transformed it into her tribute café:

        Her logo
        on the front window
        lets you know:

Norma Jean's Coffee
        Bean There, Done That

        And inside a circle
        an image of Norma Jean
        holding up high a cup of java,
        her dress billowed up,
        as in the famous photo—

        You know,
        the Marilyn photo.

But before I go on, I must add, the tribute name
was also inspired by her mother, who had, in fact,
    the name "Norma Jean."

Of course Marilyn Monroe had always been in mind
(you must know her name was originally Norma Jean)
& so, tastefully, artfully, Marilyn photos & artwork
& other icons of her era hang on the walls...

     Such as...across from
the one, long, dark wood bench,
with an equally long mirror running above the full length of it,
you face the pretty large painting "Java Dreams" by Chris Consani,
on the opposite wall, depicting an imagined coffee bar scene—
Marilyn's in a pink dress, one hand holding out an old stylish dial phone,
 headpiece held in the other,
& James Dean, barista behind the counter, pulls taut on the phone line,
Marilyn's nearly closed eyes peering coquettishly, as if to say,
 I see you reining in my line, Dean...
& Elvis sits at the bar behind Marilyn, casually, indifferently,
 looking over,
& Humphrey Bogart reads a newspaper at the bar further back.

And you see on the wall, behind the order counter,
a photo of a young Elvis, with this quote,
 I never expected to be
 anybody important.

     And here's Cathy, present day—
And Cathy? She deserves the title "Queen of Baking"—
Baking, baking, baking, she's always baking somethin'
 in the kitchen back there;
so much of what you find here she bakes herself.
Look—display platters, or down inside the glass cooler,
 or peer inside the big round jars:
She's got cheesecake, coffee cake, chocolate fudge cake, pumpkin pie
 —& any of them served up with whipped cream—,
also carrot cake, turnovers, Danish, banana bread, pumpkin bread,
muffins all kinds...lemon tarts, cinnamon rolls, brownies, macaroons,
moon pies, chocolate croissants—or croissants any way you like them—,

chocolate chip cookies, peanut butter cookies, cranberry bars,
rice krispy treats…& scones of all kinds are always the favorites
of many who come in looking for them…
How could you not find something to tempt you—?
And there's a large black menu board behind the counter:
You find listed breakfast burritos, breakfast bagels,
breakfast croissants *& sandwiches*—oh, a Norma Jean's sandwich
I'll take alright—or how about a delicious bagel & lox?—
          & there're smoothies & coffees, of course,
—drip coffees—or quick to-go coffee, & espresso drinks,
& on shelves, you see the big Ball glass jars of teas…

          And so I sat here
over the years & indulged & worked on
so many manuscripts & met so many here.
I sit here now & gaze out the window on Aptos Village—
With a coffee, a sandwich, I decided on a chocolate chip cookie,
I remember it all…& I look back at the counter & it occurs
to me again, Cathy's become the *Star of Sweet Delights*,
thinking too of the name "Norma Jean" connecting the dots
from mother to another star of the big screen,
& a once-upon-a yesteryear time…

8043 Soquel Dr, Aptos
November 5, 2016

The White Raven:
Your Mountain Town Hangout Café

Right smack in the center of Felton, right close
to the community deck where the towering landmark
redwood tree so prominently from all around you'll see,
on the long, old mountain town business strip of Highway 9,
look up above a big front window, above the awning,
an old wood plank Western town façade you'll see,
& a sign:
        The White Raven
          Coffee & Tea
         (with white raven icon)
& it's—above the other front window—:
       Home of Larry's Famous Chai
       (with white raven in upward flight)
& below that:
       The Best Little Pourhouse
          in Felton
And you find four white ravens in open-winged flight
etched on the front glass door.

                              It's the year-round
coffee & tea & chai hangout place alright,
made famous by previous owner Larry's home-brewed chai,
about the best you'll ever taste, guaranteed—
                             On rainy wintry days
the place sure gets packed & cozy, a line will start
    right at the door.
It's—as you take in that first impression—quite the quaint
& funky, oh, yes, hippyish, artsy-crafts, old mountain town feel
    of a local watering hole—
                            In other words, it has character.
The regulars from all parts around show up, almost daily,
eventually show up on some day or another,
so you eventually come to know, if you're around enough,
    pretty much who's who…

And then the tourists also come & families come,
    just about year-round,
                      always coming through town…
ever popular Henry Cowell Redwoods State Park
is just down the highway, if you didn't know.

                    Two tables out front,
favorite of good weather leisurely conversing friends,
or just kickback at one of them & it's a watch Felton life
    kind of morning or afternoon…
There're only 8 small round tables in the main room,
so the place can fill up pretty quick, once the line starts;
back room has a big round table, two cushioned chairs,
a kids' space, with stuffed animals & kids' books,
& a bookshelf for browsing, & always you find
a few books for sale on other shelves—a carryover
from older days—, & there's a big display case facing out
    of greeting cards.
There's new art on the walls 'bout every two months,
shelves of all kinds of little gift items; & jewelry, hats & caps,
T-shirts & summertime sunglasses; there're fancy bottles
& of course, all kinds'a coffee cups…
                  And Dorothy, the owner,
loves frogs, so you'll find frog critters of some kind,
hanging around, peeking out from somewhere, too.
And there's an out the back door somewhat enclosed patio,
for those who might want a quieter space.
                      Dorothy's always
changing it out in some way, at least every season,
always old stuff goes out & new stuff comes in,
but Romeo the skeleton stayed on, up in the back corner
of the main room, slouched on the top shelf there,
left over from a year ago Halloween.

                  Find eats & drinks
down in a glass display beneath the order counter,
pastries in a small plastic display, cookies in glass jars…

& there's even an old-fashioned gumball machine next
    to the front door…
& yes, the always all friendly baristas come to know you,
as you get to know them…names are freely exchanged
& usually sooner rather than later get remembered—
If you're a regular, they all know your drink,
you hardly need to say a word…

                So it's time to hang out awhile,
time for some to get on the Internet, of course,
time for some to write in a diary, work on a manuscript
    or make a sketch,
time to, like everyone used to, read a book even…
But above all, it's always time to chat with someone—
Who might you unexpectedly intersect with today?
Who new in your world might you meet?

                Dorothy knows well
the kind'a place she's got goin' here…
she knows how to foster what customers come for.

6253 Highway 9, Felton
November 2016

A Mr. Toots Evening

Yes, it's a most why-not-get-out-&-enjoy-it
    evening—

                                    And so here,
on the Esplanade, in popular Capitola-by-the-Sea,
I find myself in front of Toots,
& comes over me overwhelmingly
                                this feeling—
    I decide to walk up the carpeted steps.
It's the memory, comes over me—
It feels warm & familiar here as I take the last step;
so often I hung out & sipped a coffee or cappuccino here
many early Cruz'n, so many long years ago,
                it all comes back this moment—
I now saunter up to the sliding glass door
                        & step out the balcony—
How often too I shared this upstairs Mr. Toots view
    with a female companion.
How many over those early Cruz'n, so many long years ago—
Oh, I can't remember how many precisely.

Bordered by beach, the mouth of Soquel Creek
is summer gathered into a pool directly below;
a crescent Moon wavy reflects on the barely rippling surface;
there're leisurely ducks, gulls leisurely sailing in & out;
many a packed dinner table to the right below
                      on Margaritaville's creekside patio.
    And not a trace of fog anywhere—
A clear, calm, waning blue sweeps entire every degree of the sky;
on the horizon of Monterey, the blue mountain body of Goddess,
    how beautifully She reclines.
                            Other side the creek,
the Mediterranean picture-quaint cottages
    fade into subtle pastel colors,
& homes outline sharply against the west on the ridge
    distant the street bridge.

It is the gorgeous sensation of late summer here—
    gorgeous   gorgeous
Which is why they all come out to the Esplanade tonight.
Which is why we sat here so often shoulder to shoulder.

221 Esplanade, Capitola
August 2001

Sip Sip: Mutari Chocolate

A weekend popup, they call it,
& Mutari Chocolate, on Front St.,
has the space, this *is* the place,
to come sip sip liquid chocolate,
indulge indulge in potent, handcrafted, thick, sip sip
    sipping chocolate—
There's a little, light lit, sandwich sign
out on the sidewalk,
we come in just this side of late—

                        Soft lit place,
with little hanging lights strung across the room,
big filament yellowish bulbs glow here, there,
& little tea candles sit on square tables
& on larger tables along the wall…
& a soft, brown sofa faces a divan,
                        or,
there's a bar to sit at, if you want…
            & Stephen happens to be
the new owner, at this new location,
concocts all the chocolate drinks himself,
he's heart & soul, no doubt, into what he does here.
For chocolate sipping aficionados, this *is* the place
    in Santa Cruz…
                A stove sits
right behind the counter
heating a few small sauce pots, he's stirring
with metal spoon slowly slowly in one of them—
It's thick & dark & a bit mysterious in there…

You want a hot chocolate like you've never had before?
Or a thick thicker, sip sip only sipping chocolate?

                    These are genuinely
dark cacao chocolate concoction creations alright…

& now brought out in these small ceramic cups
on a little wood & marble serving board,
sitting in front of the three of us, Rhonda, Steve & me…
You gaze into dark brown, chocolate fullness,
it's the pleroma of chocolate…
You lift your cup & sniff…& sip…
      & you say, *Wow, this is it!*

Thick hot brown chocolate lava…sip…
complex deep forest flavored…sip…
    mouth puckering,
        coating all over your tongue…
           sip…& savor…
                rich, potent
cacao releasing neurotransmitters
              of bliss melting feeling…
      theobromine…anandamide…phenylethylamine…
        the deep, intense, sensation experience
    of true dark choc-o-late…
                Sip sip…
  oh, you're getting warm
        & buzzy fuzzy,
    a wave of so good,
      your neurons are firing
  little signals of happiness…

        And you want so much to share…
these heart-spontaneous bursts…old memories…
your gratitude, your enthusiasms…new projects…
exploring new shops…travels…smiling as you sip…
And through the big tall windows,
people back & forth on the sidewalk go,
cars stop at the traffic light, back & forth the street
    they go…

        A person or two had still come in,
a person or two finish & walk out,

      & Rhonda's at the counter asking Stephen questions,
Rhonda's endless curiosity leads to question
    after question…
                        And he gladly obliges,
shares about chocolate formulas, different drinks…
chocolate cookies, his little chocolate delicacies…
    different desserts…
& the chocolate cacao bars he'll soon be crafting…
& he knows food too, can cook up a gourmet dinner,
    he says…

                        And our returning
some other weekend, we meet his wife & partner
in this rarified handcrafted chocolate world—
Katy, all smiling & friendly, as we chat with her,
& she is so glad that we'll be back…
Oh, yes, we'll be back…

504 A Front St., Santa Cruz
January 2017

Little Café Delmarette

          And next to
the Del Mar (Theatre)
is little Café Delmarette,
a cubbyhole kind'a joint
—3 tables inside, a wood bar lookin' out
the window on Pacific Ave—
        A larger hangout space outside
with metal partition enclosure,
        like havin' a perch on the Ave—
A half dozen wood tables out here...
It's a perfect little watering hole on a casual day—
Are you in a rush? Do you need to be
    in a rush?
               Stop, have a bite—
Grill-styled tasty sandwiches,
good veggie creamed or roasted soup de jour,
good jumpstart espresso, mochas...
homemade syrups even...

                And there's
people back & forth cruz'n along,
always cruz'n along
            on the Ave...
So a good place for people watchin'
& street photo studies, if you're into that—
So many characters, so many vignettes,
you would never be able to capture them all—
But you can sit here awhile & eat & drink
    & watch it all...

You, like a bird perched on the Ave,
you've got eyes on the Ave—

And Go Ask Alice is across the street...

1126 Pacific Ave, Santa Cruz
March 2017

Go Ask Alice

From the outside
it's not really clear what's
going on
        inside.

              Go ahead, take a trip,
& walk in. It's a big space inside.
It's a throwback to…like a Sixties shop,
but lots bigger, tidier, classier
        —upscaled, like everything is today.
A life-size Johnny Depp Mad Hatter smiles at'cha
to your right, his hand raised, fingers pinching
    the rim of his hat,
& as you walk in a little further—you've already begun
to follow the checkerboard path back at the door
starting up the near wall winding across the floor—,
three young gal manikins in cool fashion stare blank
behind a table with books & two cushioned chairs…
So you follow the checkerboard path into the store,
which will take you to a hobbit door further in
    on the wall.   And you're surrounded by
Alice in Wonderland full wall murals—
Colors, colors galore, bright leafy green colors
& mushrooms, MUSHROOMS of color,
& flowers…& a butterfly & the Cheshire smiling cat
    is sittin' up in a twisty tree…

              And one of the Alice's
behind the counter—there're all Alices here—
said, referring to recent years of the moneyed,
yuppified Cruz,
    It's not the Santa Cruz I used to know,
    when I came here as a kid.

*We're about bringing back a piece
of old school Santa Cruz,
like it used to be...*

                       And lots'a stuff—
Large psychedelic & artsy design tapestries,
clothes racks, scarves, leather belts & hats by Subverse,
    proudly made in The Cruz...
all kinds'a bagged herbs along a wall, bottles of herbs,
& more heady trippy ones kept behind the counter...
& tinctures for libido & mellowness & sweet dreams,
kava chocolate bars, nutritional chocolates,
essential oils, sage smudging sticks & wands,
candles, incense, stickers, dreamcatchers,
here you see colorful hula hoops...
& necklaces, anklets & other jewelry,
little banners, decals, a table of Tarot,
oracle & rune cards, figurines here & there,
& then a few dressing rooms in back...
And a kava bar in front is in the works...
oh, & a psychic reading table is set up.

                Ask Alice & she will say,
Wanna go back down the rabbit hole?
Yes, it's a throwback to a Sixties reconstructed scene
    in the 2000 teens...
sort of an anachronism, but, hey, The Cruz
always has a place in its heart for its old Cruz'n past,
and right here, where it belongs, on the Ave...

1125 Pacific Ave., Santa Cruz
March 19, 2017

Pergolesi is Closing

It will take a while to sink in.
You might have heard: Pergolesi is closing—
Yes, Caffé Pergolesi. Closing. Shut. And that's it.
The Pergolesi era in The Cruz will be over.
    Can you believe?

Caffé Pergolesi,
in the 19th Century Victorian funky Dr. Miller's Building,
on Cedar St. since the mid-1980s—
    Pergolesi is closing.
Caffé Pergolesi,
originally first opening in 1973 in the red brick building
that collapsed in the great Quake of '89 in the courtyard behind
the old Pacific Ave location of Bookshop Santa Cruz—
    Pergolesi is closing.
Caffé Pergolesi,
a bohemian Cruz'n institution, a UC student tradition,
a local landmark of hang-out coffee drinking, of good eats & sweets—
    Pergolesi is closing.
Caffé Pergolesi,
a place to kick back for hours, a place to rendezvous
with a friend, a business partner, a date, a lover, a trysting place,
a place mobbed by friends—
    Pergolesi is closing.
Caffé Pergolesi,
a place to study, write, read a book, conduct meetings,
brainstorm, a host of how many poetry readings over the years—
    Pergolesi is closing.
Caffé Pergolesi,
of loud metal & punk & hard rock, of techno rock,
blastin' from behind the serving counter the moment you walked in—
    Pergolesi is closing.
Caffé Pergolesi,
where punker skinhead & hippie dreadlock interfaced,
where bearded old timers sat amidst all the naïve young student souls—
    Pergolesi is closing.

Caffé Pergolesi,
where artists, writers, poets, misfits, eccentrics, wanderers,
left field thinkers, transgender marginals, all found sanctuary—
    Pergolesi is closing.

                              Tables outside
to both sides the tight-spaced concrete & wood steps,
its throwback era wood porch & bench to lounge
with elbows propped, watch all the so hip & cool selfie-conscious
    make their way up the steps...
The deep maroon walls surrounding back of the counter,
menu boards behind, main room of fireplace, mantle & mirror
above it seemingly out of place in this Postmodern, heavy urban-feel,
    diversity land—
Green sofa, cushioned chairs, a few Persian throw rugs hiding patches
of old linoleum, worn flower-patterned carpeted slightly uneven
floored rooms to both sides the main room,
the always taken church pew study table, those dancing naked
angel babies painted under the twirling blades of the high ceiling fan,
& that dark-walled, graffiti-plastered, barebones bathroom...

    *

It's just before 7pm, Friday, 2 days before final closing day
& it's packed inside, the porch packed, about to start this evening
the live loud heavy metal, hard rock, 8 bands on the program,
the whole left side room had been cleared out for the bands
    & crowd,
               it was getting pretty tight in there...
and the line at the counter was goin' out the door.
And when the music started, it was standing room only...
And was it loud, slamming loud, heads all pointed,
some banging, to the band, couldn't make out a single word
    in the deafening sound.
A few had cameras, a few took smart phone photos.
I soon had my fill. To imagine the rest of that evening...

And tomorrow evening, scheduled again, another round
of 3 bands, a grand finale before the final closing.

*

Saturday afternoon, the 26th of August 2017,
the last day of The Perg, & Rhonda & I come to sit
& have a coffee & take in the vibes & reminisce
& appreciate the years Pergolesi had sailed with The Cruz.
    I take photos, a few notes.
Karl Heiman, owner the last 14 years,
comes walking through & smiles as we notice him
& thank him for his time as captain of this motley cruise.
He has assured everyone Mr. Toots Coffeehouse in Capitola
(he is also owner of) he will keep in business.
    No issue there.

And prices this last day he's thrown way back to
    1973…

418 Cedar St., Santa Cruz
August / December 2017

Storefront Logos Still

                      So this storefront
vacancy still remains the face of the once
well-known Logos, the biggest, best, used bookstore
    in Santa Cruz—
Actually it had new, used & rare books, & records,
    CDs & DVDs.
Here it is, sitting closed now for 3 years,
a not forgotten presence that had so popular
    of a past.
The prominent red door overhang still says
in letters & numbers in white, Logos 1117 Logos—
    1117 Pacific Avenue, that is.
Posters on the windows announce a new business
—a brewery—but was supposed to go in already
back in 2019…so the space still remains suspended in time.
Windows are covered but you can look through
the glass doors into a cavernous, vacuous, interior.
A memory comes of all those books…to think,
it was a once busy, thriving bookstore.

This is what remains of the Logos of memories…
How many books had I purchased here over the years.
How many times browsing through the shelves…
    & it had an extensive downstairs.
How many times was I inspired on the spot
by a book I chanced upon…by so many books.
How many times encountering friends here,
how many times rendezvousing with friends—
Show up at Logos, I'll be browsing there.

To see its storefront still is sad.
The memories of its heyday won't go away.

October 4, 2020

Taqueria Vallarta

It's gotten to be the most popular easy eatin'
    Mexican place around—
Low-priced, good tastin', plenty on the plate,
people come in waves & line up to the counter,
    order takers are always ready,
they got the big menu spread above,
& they're cookin' & preparin' pretty fast back there,
servers are always callin' out numbers—
They bring the plate right to ya.

There're two murals cover entire opposite walls,
big TV always playin' never audible
in the upper left corner
    —some Mexican station always playin'—,
ceiling fans are always spinnin',
there're these simple domed lights hangin' down,
one piece swivel-seat tables firmly secured
    to the floor—
             It's your basic,
with a lotta people walkin' in,
lotta standin' round for takeout,
lotta friends, families, lotta little groups,
lotta my girlfriend/your boyfriend,
    lotta talkin',
always a lotta eatin'
    goin' on.

608 Soquel Ave, Santa Cruz
August 2000

Rio is Dead...*but*—

Old Santa Cruz landmark Rio,
in red lettering against green, looks quite done in—
It's Friday night & all the lights are out, it's ghostly,
here are no big flashy movie posters out on display,
the little silvery metal of a box office is vacant,
think that someone used to work in there every night,
kind'a haunted feelin' now, the alcove, like, all dirty lookin'
    the way places get when abandoned.
I remember when *ET* once played here for weeks on end,
I remember when there would be a line around the corner,
people slipped into the Oasis Café there & got drinks—
That too is gone, now a Mexican restaurant, Jalapeños.

Up on the marquee, you can't miss it though,
drivin' up Seabright, it's right there in your face—
Blank otherwise, there's one last statement
someone's assembled up there
to make to all the world,

        CAPITALISM KILLS

& so apparently it has...

1205 Soquel Ave, Santa Cruz
June 2000

And here it is, late in the year December,
I'm drivin' by & it's kind of a surprise, to see,
up there, on its long neglected marquee,

        THE RIO IS ALIVE

What? Come back to life?
So I park & get out & read
that it's undergoing this transformation
into this multipurpose live performance venue
& arts space & movie theatre, all-in-one.
      Now isn't that somethin'?
Perhaps a new kind'a capitalism has learned
      resuscitation.

December 2000

Now *The Union*

Let's change the name too—
So now it's called "120 Union"
—which is simply its address—,
or, simply, as it goes by now *The Union*—
And you got people lookin' at you, like, what?
    The Union?
        Where's that?
            Never heard of it—
But if you say, *Used to be, ya know,*
    the Jahva House,
            it's like,
Oh, yes, I know the place.
So it's The Union now?

Yes, it has changed names—changed hands—,
as so often happens on this changin' Cruz,
but it's basically your same, big, sharp-echoing,
    high-raftered place
—same ol' warehouse once kind'a place—,
still another one of your coffee drinkin'
of a popular hangout kind'a place,
    downtown S. Cruz.
It's where Synergy Party last year
    got started,
but, then, what's, like, happened with that now?
Oh, well, another on The Cruz venture...they come
    & they go...

Got'ta say, they've got the quirky art stuff kind'a look—
For awhile they had an old phone booth
    in the middle of the place
with a busted computer monitor & all this wiring inside;
there're usually some huge provocative or at least striking
    in-some-way paintings

      hangin' somewhere,
like now they're over the long, curvy round counter
  & on a couple of the walls;
& look at these huge, & I mean huge, artsy urns,
must take half a dozen muscle guys to budge 'em,
  maybe even a crane;
& there's this junk metal assembled sort'a dragonfly
  hoverin' overhead;
that streetlight I would say kind'a out'a place hangin' horizontal,
with floodlights mounted along it for performance events,
you look up, it's, like, right in your face, seems out'a some
  sci fi movie;
    & there's that multiple tree level display case
now an art statement stocked with dozens
of cheap mass market cupcakes & donuts & pastry sweets inside—
they must be, like, rock solid hard, you'd think, preserved
  in their own artificial gunk;
& the big black grand piano is still there;
& the tall glass entry doors have replaced
  the fold out heavy wooden one—
The new ones simply get propped open
  during hours of business.   And the sign outside
with the big-lettered art deco name "Union"
seems like it belongs in a big city somewhere,
you might even expect a bar, perhaps, the way it looks.
But, as the music of the Grateful Dead is playin'
  this moment,
    on this pleasant, kick-back afternoon,
there's a clear hint of the Jahva House past.

120 Union, Santa Cruz
September/December 2003

And today I read on the door,
    July of '05,
To our valued customers:
Thank you for all your support.
120 Union Café is now closed.

    And so it goes—
They will open again
as *Coastline*: an organic brewpub restaurant.
And so it goes,
this perpetual font

    of *change, change, change...*

Felix Kulpa Gallery

You walk thru this pull-away gateway painted black
into a little curvy walkway sculpture garden
      bordered with virgin white stones—
                      In front of you immediately
lots of sweet alyssum, geraniums & other flowers
round a raised funky fountain basin a central pillar goin' up,
a melted monitor of some kind'a way outdated technology
    on top,
with water trickling down from on top of that;
& there's an old television set up high on some metal framework,
a motorcycle made of junk metal, there's one of those huge art urns
    you used to see at the old Union café,
                    & an old phone booth you see,
water trickling down over the phone inside,
& I can't help thinkin' again of the old Union café;
                      & of course
that big parking lot light just lyin' there on its side
    makes me think of the old Union too.
And as I'm walkin' inside the gallery itself, the art funk guitars,
    there on display,
        made of a shovel & a wheel well
              & this square piece'a somethin',
        & you know, I now think I was right—
lots of this stuff found its way here from the old Union.
                      And Isaac behind the desk
says he used to host the open mikes there,
    (which I had never managed on Mondays
      to get to,
    otherwise I would have recognized him too).
                      And then I discover
    —as I stopped here another time—,
talking this time with the owner Robbie Schoen,
that he was considered the artist-in-residence
    at the old Union.

        Things do come around again.

    And now
I'll look at
        the new art.

107 Elm St. Santa Cruz
September 2006

41st Avenue Shop Shop Shop

He remembered a time, he said,
when a stop sign
was pretty much obscured
by the tall weeds at the corner of Capitola Road
    & 41st Avenue—
                Can you believe?
    How many years ago must that have been?
(He had told me this already some 25 years ago;
  I hadn't thought of asking him how far further back
    he meant.)
Thing is, it's been *the* major shopping intersection
    of the whole county,
            ever since I arrived,
                      & that was back in '76,
      each quadrant, in fact,
boasts a whole shopping blitz of its own—
Premier, of course, is the big Capitola Mall, your classic, enclosed,
dedicated utterly to an absolute shopping experience of a mall—
Entering on 41st Avenue, you're greeted by the two classy, night-lit,
    ground level marquees angled on each side,
the big, nearly continuous parking lots going all around,
        come Christmas season you'll find them all full
    (& gulls, for some reason, you'll always see here circling about)—
Sears at one end been there forever, Mervyn's the other end,
used to be JC Penny in the back but now Macy's is in there,
    & Gottshalks is also there in the back,
& how many dozens of other businesses you'll find in there too,
    with so many over the years come & gone.
        (You walk up 41st Avenue in front of the Mall
    & you'll see our tallest peak Loma Prieta on the far distant right
            above buildings across the street, between the trees...
And of course there's a business strip alongside a side parking lot,
a Ross Dress For Less there, a Pacific Gas & Electric office,
    a Vitamin Center, & others,
& there're still loads of shopping businesses & restaurants

  all along Clares Street behind all those
    that went in some number of years ago—

    And across Capitola Road
used to be called, or am I wrong?
  King's Plaza, if I remember—
        Or am I wrong?
You don't see any identifying marquee anywhere
—which is quite unusual, an anomaly in the very center
of all this—I thought there had been a name to all this.
Some King's Court bar, I remember, used to be in there,
perhaps where the whole shopping center I thought
  had got its name from,
    but that bar's long gone—
      Now,
there's some jewelers in there, a hair salon,
& a well-known Monterey Bay area photo business—
  Bay Photo Lab,
replaced some eating place, if I remember correctly,
  next to the bar.
The marquee that you do see out along Capitola Road
  lists movies for the 41st Avenue Cinemas,
    back in the corner next to Capitola Book Café,
& Tony & Alba's Pizza just across from it has been there awhile now,
along with Camera Club/Palace Art & Office Supply/Pet Emporium/
  & Pretty Mama clothing all going that one row,
& the row continuing with Capitola Book Café, itself being
  a well-known tradition here
—new book-signing authors are always coming through here—,
you also find a Rite Aid pharmacy, an Albertsons supermarket,
  & then other businesses goin' down & round the corner,
    like Kragen Auto Parts, the last one that's in there.
And then at the row of businesses back toward Capitola Road
  where the marquee is
you find a Baskin Robbins ice cream parlor, Orchard Supply Hardware,
See's Candies on the corner—,
      all seem to have been there awhile,

    & round the side facing Capitola Road itself, Erik's Deli Café,
        an old Santa Cruz small franchise classic,
reminds you something of The Cruz's funkier days,
        like it was back in the 70s.
And there's generic Tiny's Family Restaurant
in a niche of its own right on 41st there.

    Then,
across from Capitola Mall, on 41st, once you look passed
the imposition of the monumental brown monstrosity World Savings
you see a more recent glitzy makeover look Capitola Station—
        (& two very tall, slender palms you'll see behind, in the distance,
            & offset from them, a third,
        & there, again, in the distance, all-seeing Loma Prieta…
A MacDonald's is in there, music store Wherehouse been there awhile,
Longs Drugs been there a long time, & there's some chain supermarket,
Ralphs now—where did that name come from—isn't that from LA?
Different names have come & gone there, it seems.
                      And on that corner is a Wells Fargo Bank,
which faces off from a Bank of America on the Capitola Mall corner
with its big 20-foot-tall windows & cement pillars going up
to the overhang of brown roof, the Wells Fargo lookin' quite modest
    in comparison.
                    It is curious, isn't it,
two banks face off, side by side corners,
& opposite them, two gas stations face off, Chevron & Shell,
    side by side the other corners—
Two banks & two gas stations define the major intersection
of shopping mania for this small county,
                oh, but even more than that—
Banks & gas stations have come to define the life of us all,
    have they not,
        here in the USA?

And kitty-corner from the big Capitola Mall
—and that'll be behind the Chevron Station on the corner,
there's a smaller Wind & Sea Plaza
        —you could easily miss the modest marquee there—.

Since when has Graceland Christian Books been back in there?
(Behind this plaza, next driveway down Capitola Rd, you'll find
    the Department of Motor Vehicles.)
And going further down 41st that same side the street
an office building an old company I used to work for was in there,
& then you find the Four Star Center, another little shopping world,
a Little Caesars Pizza in there (didn't that franchise originate
    back in my hometown, Detroit, or no?)
Across the street here, if you look, you'll see a Best Western motel.
You find a business office next—the 41st Avenue Plaza building,
then the Twin Palms offices with the absolutely perfect pair of palms
    out in front,
                  Life Spring Fellowship church, again, across the way,
& further down there's even yet another shopping plaza
    —Begonia Plaza—
                        before you reach the railroad tracks,
a New Leaf Community Market a Santa Cruz healthy food type store
    next Way of Life is in there,
& next up, the Spa Fitness Center building,
& across the avenue just before the tracks, that big, brown brick
    O'Neill Surf Shop you'll see
                  framed by palms,
                              & there're restaurants
& small local businesses & other office plazas
    goin' block after block,
including bicycle shops, insurance, tax service, American Dream Realty,
Florabunda Nursery & Florist, & a whole bank of second hand shops,
&, oh, so many others, goin' both sides 41st all the way
    to Portola Drive,
            where, 'cept for the little shopping corner there,
it's then residential all the way to East Cliff Drive,
which curves right there along the Bay
            —the Pleasure Point area
it's always been called,
& there's a history to that name.

            And going back down 41st
the other direction from Capitola Mall

—that's back toward Highway 1—, you find more banks
    —you might have figured, there're all over in this area—,
a Lyons Restaurant, Blockbuster Video, Pacific Vetenary Specialists,
some mattress store crossing Clares Street, some car wash,
    the cooking grease you'll smell of KFC,
there's the Housing Authority of the County of Santa Cruz building,
a 76 gas station—actually there're two, angled across from each other
    on both sides the street—,
& starting back on the other side again, a Burger King on corner
    of Clares,
        then a small complex of offices/businesses,
a Men's Warehouse next this big orange brick concave façade
    that just says in big letters *Liquor*,
        with a Del Mar Cleaners next to it,
           & next to that in big letters, simply *Wash Dry*.
    And of course
down at the highway entrance south side again
are the back-to-back dealerships of Capitola Auto Mall,
which I do have my own memories of, back in the mid-80s,
since I sat in my car many a night back then
    protecting the place,
as it was under construction.
        Then, across the highway
—on the overpass bridge, there's distant Loma Prieta
    as visible as could be, crowning the top ridge,
        with all these antennas sprouting on top of it—,
it's a Big K-Mart you see across the highway there, a Safeway next to it,
    both set way back of a big big parking lot,
& there's a USA gas station, other eating places & other businesses,
& back next to the highway, again, opposite side the avenue,
    is San Lorenzo Lumber, well-known in the county,
& after that, more small businesses & another couple restaurants,
    —even a Psychic Shop you'll find along there—,
& 41st ends then at Soquel Drive, with businesses there too
    all along in both directions,
           going north & going south.

Yes, everyone in the county knows 41st Avenue—

You get to know it quickly enough, as the county of Santa Cruz
    is just about the smallest in the state there is.
Nearly everything you might imagine shopping for is here,
    on one long drive of shop shop shop.

                          From birth on
just about everyone in America undergoes
the thorough mental conditioning & desire encoding
to want & want more & more & more material things & services
    & consumables,
our world now epitomized as Shop Shop Shop Buy Buy Buy
    Spend Spend Spend,
              & all woven so thoroughly into television, radio,
magazines, newspapers, financial institutions, the credit system,
into industry, manufacturing, Wall Street & Madison Avenue
    New York,
all of this woven into image & status & life style,
                    the whole yearly consumer cycle
culminating in the manic month-long buying blitz
    we all know as the Christmas season,
all paying homage to the economic monster, ruling all—
    Capitalism,
        & its god,
                the Almighty Dollar,
    or simply, let us say,
                    MONEY.

Shop Shop Shop Buy Buy Buy Spend Spend Spend—
And don't we all know it, our citizens simply take it
    for granted,
after all, this is what Human Reality has evolved to,
above all, in the mainstream current of America,
    yes, it's all very well established here,
        Santa Cruz the Weird is no exception.
    Let's be honest about it—
Materialism, consumerism, capitalism,
    now just about dominate the planet,

& not everyone, not every society, not every country,
    is pleased about it.
Now to actually sit down & make the effort
    to write a poem about all this,
with all these details that name names & say what's where,
    what we find has defined our streets—
It's all just so ordinary, so everyday, so all-surrounding us,
why would a poet want to write about
                                 the obvious?

August 2004

Pizza My Heart

I'm sittin' eatin' this Maui Wowie of a good-sized, mouth-watering slice
in this popular pizza joint, its memorabilia of surfer photos all nicely framed
    & mounted, plastered up on every wall,
shiny polished surfboards mounted & hangin' down the ceiling,
& young guys & gals queue up in a ritual lookin' down pointin' through the glass,
a motley assortment of big V slices spread out there that by-the-slice
    made a name for this place—
                        Whole pies they got cookin' up in these wide,
stacked up, narrow-door ovens, like they're openin' & shuttin' nonstop.
It's packed in here, they're all sittin' in these royal rust-stain wooden booths,
    & I'm thinkin' what an alien world this is I find myself in—
I swear I'm from elsewhere, but for now, I'm sittin' here, playin' as best I can
at bein' second nature to all this what they call the business of livin', as humans do,
    like, gettin' a bite.

Oh, such a chameleon I am, whatever the element, I blend in,
like I'm watchin' out the window persons like a moving picture streamin' by,
Pacific Avenue the title, directly across the old Cruz classic Logos Used Books—
And she walks by, oh, she who just happened to catch my eye
    —I think, I know how to walk like that too—.
Not a single person around registers in the memory bank though,
the way they come & go on The Cruz, you don't see all you used to know.
Oh, such a good chameleon I am, I get nothin' so much as a blink
    out of anyone—

                And just like that,
it's quieting down already—
Well, it's Sunday, and it's the early darkness of November settling in…
This last bit of crust I just don't think I'll eat.

1116 Pacific Ave, Santa Cruz
November 14, 2004

The Farmers' Scene

    What a scene, what a scene,
what a tradition goin' of a little community-building scene all its own—
Every Wednesday afternoon, you know, it's the Farmers' Market,
    here, downtown, in Santa Cruz style,
it's poppin' popular like, as you can see for yourself—

Three modest aisles of primarily white pointy—a few blue
    & a few red—
        canopied booths & back-ended vehicles & tables you see
            as you approach,
snug in the one block back from Pacific Ave, a parking lot here
    that's back behind Logos Used Books & Toadal Fitness,
        alongside Cedar St—
All the famously—the greater bulk of it—organically grown produce
you'll find here as you stop & go from booth to booth—
                        Small farms
from up the north county coast & from right here in Santa Cruz
& from south of town Corralitos & Watsonville way,
all through the rich agricultural Pajaro Valley & from over the summit,
    Los Gatos there;
           & from Hollister
& San Juan Bautista down in neighboring San Benito county;
from Brentwood in Contra Costa; from Oakdale, Turlock, Modesto
    & Fresno,
        coming in all the way from the Central Valley,
they all bring us such delicious & wholesome, directly from-the-farm
    fresh produce—
                Oh, what a scene, what a scene,
to saunter through leisurely as you stop & look & squeeze
& try a sample of this, that, or the other,
& you run into so many friends & old friends, like, so-and-so
you haven't seen in how long? & those you see here every week;
and it's quite the casual place & time to rendezvous
    with one of your friends,
as you're out shopping your Farmers' Market.

                              Oh, such an abundance
we have here, so much luscious, fresh-from-the-Earth,
simply good & natural, so much organic food here—
Can we say we are so lucky?
                              What is it you want?
Like corn on the cob? Looks good—
Want beans? —There're all kinds'a beans—look
at that mountain of green beans on that table over there—
Need lettuce? —Oh, there're bins of all sorts of leafy greens.
You want carrots, cucumbers, squash, zucchini, beets, radishes,
    asparagus, cabbage, cauliflower, celery—?
                              What about spinach?
      Need cilantro, dill, or parsley? Like fennel?
                              Dandelions for your salad?
    Want peas in the pod?
            Need potatoes? So many different kinds'a potatoes here—
What about tomatoes? What about these little cherry tomatoes?
You see some farms boast about their prized heirloom seeds.
What about garlic or onions—you need some kind'a onions?
    What about bell peppers?
There comes the season for chili peppers too—all kinds'a them—
    How hot do you want 'em?
                And broccoli, eggplant, chard, bok choy, kale—
                      You want brussels sprouts on the stem?
    What about avocadoes?
                         —Wow, not many left this week.
        Give 'em a squeeze—
                Not real hard, not too soft, just right, right?
And don't forget the artichokes—
                         Here we live,
right smack on the central coast of the state,
where almost literally all the artichokes of the world are grown
            —who can say Castroville?—;
& we get 'em right here.
                    Or you want freshly cut flowers?
    There're plenty of them to choose from.
What about herbs growing all neatly in their little trays?
                    You want melons—all kinds'a melons—,

   what about big hunky watermelons?
What about oranges, kiwi, grapefruit, or lemons?
The season for cherries & blueberries sure goes by fast—
     And what about apricots, kumquats or them loquats?
         And look here—
There're nectarines & luscious dark plums,
   & peaches
     Peaches
      PEACHES—!!
You're handed a wedge of a peach on a skewer, and—
 Wow, they're the sweetest I've ever tasted—
       Sweetest & juiciest ever.
   That's it, you're sold.
You wanna try a slice of the oranges? They're over there—
They got ice-cold pomegranate juice too—& it's good.
      Of course, look at all the strawberries—
Baskets & baskets of 'em, there're whole bins of 'em;
  you know the Watsonville area is famous
    for its strawberries—
Yep, the best I've ever tasted, you don't get 'em any better than this.
And here are little baskets too of blackberries & raspberries—
Of course you got deep purple grapes or the light green grapes,
  by the bunches;
the Central Valley, you know, really has the grapes.
        As you can see,
  it's just barely starting the season for apples now—
   Look at them apples, as they say,
        & you'll be sayin',
     & there'll be loads of 'em too—
Isn't Watsonville also famous for its apples?
(Though you hear there are fewer & fewer orchards out there every year.)
      And then come in the pears—
  It'll be apples & pears & pears & apples soon.
And late in the year there'll be all kinds of wintertime produce.

       And still—
You walk past booths of mushrooms & eggs & nuts,
dried fruit & dates, flavored almonds—

                    Are you into wheat grass? sprouts?
              What about tofu or tempeh?
Here is a table of dried kinds of crispy sea plants—
     They're nicely sea salty & tasty.
                         Or want somethin' special for lunch?
What about nori special rolls at this table here?
     Or these rice paper rolls?
                         RK (as we know him) sells 'em
              at his table here—
     And I'll tell you,
I know for a fact they're quite good—oh, they're actually
     quite delicious.
              And you'll find really good breads, cheeses, fresh fish, oysters
         —I understand Bill The Oyster Man is well-known here—;
& there's one booth's got organic-fed chickens & grass-fed beef.
              And you'll also find
         the sweets of pastries, pies,
                    —oh, there's quiche at that booth too—,
     & the exquisitely fine, handcrafted Donnelly Chocolates,
              I hear has made a name for itself worldwide;
& there's a whole table over there lined with rows & rows of jars of honey—
Oh, there're jars & bottles of all kinds'a homemade sauces & syrups
     at some booth.
And booths in a row you find of Indian, Italian & Mexican foods,
some, ready to eat on the spot, if you want.

              Yep, what a scene, what a scene,
it's a small world of a scene all its own—
It's certainly a little vortex of its own within the swirling downtown
     greater Vortex of The Cruz—
All the organic, vegan, alternative green, permaculture, hemp hippy crowd
     loves the Farmers';
the old counter-culture & rave-going crowd, they all show up here;
     & performance artists of some kind are always
         at the fringes of this—
there's always some guitarist, or your odd a cappella group
     as you find standin' here today, piping their voices—;
         & balloon lady Tarnosaurus entertains the kids this season;

& there's the full-on drumming starts up come the good weather
    back in a certain part of the parking lot, off to the side,
       it'll be quite obvious—
Someone's always bound too to have a didgeridoo, or a sax or violin
    or guitar there;
               of course you hear the tambourines;
& there's wild, red-haired Alan "Sitar" Brown
brings out at times his monster of an instrument,
about the only one around town who can really play the thing.

What it always comes down to, though, here at the Farmers',
is that cornucopia out-pouring, how it's happenin' every week,
this beautiful abundance they provide for us all of fresh, wholesome,
    produce
         right-off-the-farm
that'll always be at the heart of it all.

July 2005

Food Not Bombs

Why are all those people gathered there?

—Well, they're hungry.

Hanging from the trunk of a sycamore tree,
a sign you will see, *Food Not Bombs*—
And it's every Saturday & Sunday, 4-6 pm,
you'll see them lined up & gathered there—
                                  Food Not Bombs
sets up at the corner, Water & Front Streets,
alongside the downtown Santa Cruz Post Office
& offers freely & compassionately, no one turned away,
deliciously & genuinely healthy food to the homeless & hungry,
feeding those in need, & doing so at this same location ever since
    the Occupy Movement of 2011.
And line up they do, down the sidewalk, going even beyond
the ugly chain-link fence that first went up, but is now
a permanent, imposing, black-painted iron pointy fence
the city determined it had to put up to protect the PO,
as up to 300 people can show up for a meal over the two days—
They patiently wait in line holding big compostable
hard paper bowls, queueing up to long white folding tables
under a big, white, portable canopy, these silver hotel trays
    packed with food,
8 servers scooping out great tasting vegan dishes
—after all, it's all cooked at India Joze,
    it has to be good,
& I can attest, I indulged a bit myself—,
there's variety, there's bean chowder, fresh produce,
baked goodies, breads cut up, & a water dispenser...
They all load up & chow down sitting along the fence,
or on the lower PO steps, or wherever there's enough
    of a ledge to sit & eat...
                                  And a few
of the inner circle of friends sit on folding chairs
around the literature table—friendly Keith McHenry,

point man for this local chapter of Food Not Bombs,
    among them.

Bicycles, shopping carts, skateboards, day packs,
big black bags of personal life belongings that have been
    wheeled around
are parked along the fence, all around in the area—
A guitar or two is strummed by someone or another,
a joint or two is lit up, small conversations but more so
    silent, private, focusing on eating;
and a few latecomers are still showing up...

                  And I met
Keith McHenry when I first arrived,
he happens to be an original co-founder with 7 other
anti-nuclear activists of Food Not Bombs back in Boston
in 1980 when he was a Boston University student—
                He saw so much good
organic produce from the health food store
he worked at tossed out & wasted, what a terrible shame
that was...so he thought of sharing it with those going without,
starting at the local public housing project, why not?
And it so happened that across the street from it
—believe it or not—had gone up a new weapons lab
in the U.S. intercontinental nuclear bomb program,
which made him so immediately aware of the menace
of nuclear weapons & nuclear power...

            And he & his activist friends said
something like, *Why not offer food rather than bombs?*
So Food Not Bombs was born; & so they distributed food
to various housing projects & then offered food
—even cooked meals—directly on the street...

                Keith himself
had gone through a homeless period in the 70s,
so he had firsthand experience of what that was like.
And at some point in the 80s he migrated to San Francisco
& helped start up another Food Not Bombs group;

the homeless situation in SF was well-known
    & definitely escalating.
And for the good work of feeding the homeless there,
but without a permit, they started getting arrested—
the first arrests, including McHenry,
occurred at Golden Gate Park, August 15, 1988,
& over the years as Food Not Bombs chapters popped up
across the country their volunteers have been arrested
for the simple act of feeding the hungry thousands
    of times…

                      In Santa Cruz
a chapter was founded in 1992 by Kim Argula,
Robert Flory & Tony Mellow & others.
And McHenry came down to The Cruz
& is today spokesperson for our local Food Not Bombs.
Something like 38 years he's been dedicated to feeding
the homeless & hungry; locally he's been butting heads
with the city & a few residents who take issue
with feeding the homeless in this, as they say,
eyesore messy, openly public way.

                But, as Keith says,
We can end homelessness if we divert some
of the billions spent for war on real national security
of jobs, affordable housing, education and healthcare.
Blaming the homeless for their condition is clearly
    not working.

                Food Not Bombs
is now active in a thousand cities
in 65 countries.

And every Saturday & Sunday, 4-6 pm,
they come for the nourishment of good food,
good food served up with compassion…

September 2018/March 2019

Remember that Comedy Scene?

                                    For a few months,
that summer season, a weekly comedy scene
was happenin' at the Santa Cruz Coffee Roasting,
in the front of the place, where I'm now standin'
            —they've remodeled a bit since, I see—,
  year 2003, late summer it was,
when Rich Stimbra—Little Richie Stimbra he called himself—,
    & his San Francisco Comedy College troupe
& all manner of wannabe and seasoned stand-up comedians locally here,
& there's one or two among them might still make it big someday,
Sundays, early evenings, remember? they had the place up front here
    packed,
                all this wild goin' on & out front hoppin' on Pacific Ave,
people listenin' from the booths, sittin' packed in on the stools
& standin' at the black partition bar here, all this standin' around
    in the aisle,
kind'a loud it got, rowdy at times, always pushin' the envelope of risqué
      —you know how comics are these days—,
it got to be too much, someone thought, for the general public
passing through—young ears got to hearin' way too much,
                      apparently the word got back—
so the place had to shut Little Richie down—

                      I myself performed
a couple 5-minute stints that 2003 sudden hot summer
—I was the outsider, you know, I wasn't certified with a degree
    or anything
            to be a funny guy,
    I was more the quirky skit artist type,
but I was possessed, called myself *The Multi Guy*, a second time around
    (after year 2000),
a really kind'a bouncin' off the walls, crazy person I was that silly season,
I was even thinkin' 'bout becoming a full-time comic myself—
    Wow, that was a silly notion—

It's what happens though when your multidimensional Self,
your own shape-shifting potential Bigger Self,
                    throws out another shape for you to be,
I who discovered my many-in-one Selfhood super-creativity,
in another one of these just made for self-explorin', short-lived,
    Cruz'n scenes.

1330 Pacific Ave, Santa Cruz
October 2005

The E3: A Short Story

So soon but a memory already?
    Once again, it happens—
                        The E3 PlayHouse
had only opened in 2006, month of February,
offering another much-needed performance venue
    on the downtown scene,
and here, already, this last summer of '07, its doors have closed—
Wes Anthony, the owner, thought perhaps he could outwit
the City Planning Department, as he never, supposedly,
    as the official story goes,
filed all the exactly proper paperwork & appropriate fees
necessary to stay open late for loud music & dancing & serving drinks,
as any other late night venue does; or possibly, he was not allowed to
    because of certain zoning restrictions.
Now who can say? Wes claimed he did follow up & did make
something of an effort to resolve it— But did he really or didn't he?
There were such conflicting views...

                        Like the Pied Piper
—with a clarinet—he led a troupe of loyal supporters
down the streets to city hall for a final stand-off.
It was, as it had come out, a series of noise complaints
from an alleged someone or two living in the newly built
1010 Pacific Apartments that rubbed right up against
    the E3
that initiated the whole proceedings against him,
& then the allegation that Wes was slyly trying to elude
local ordinances & set up his own rules.

                        And so I walk this day
alongside this nondescript long cinder block solid, its solid cubes
of glass embedded, of a building that's next to where the old
Pontiac Grill used to be (it's now Café La Vie) peeking through
the silvery glassy door & I see that everything inside

has been totally stripped out,
and I can't help but think now how the E3 got its start—

Wes Anthony, kickin' around the jazz music scene
   of The Cruz
          & parts round California for years,
had arrived back in town from his Southern—Mississippi—roots
with a big stash—was an inheritance apparently that he would use
to manifest a bold business concept—

          It was:
             The E3 PlayHouse:
          Entertainment, Education, Eatery
  Its logo:
          A white hand, 3 fingers splayed,
             index finger bent over the thumb, making an e—
        the distinct E3 hand against background blue.

        Was such a perfect space this venue,
in its always seemingly dimly lit atmosphere,
its black walls with portraits of jazz greats, a bar & all its tables
   with little candles—
Had a raised black stage, the steps of which so many of us
walked up & down over the weeks & months of that first year—
Oh, all the folk singers that came through town & different kind'a bands,
the comedy shows & belly dancing, Danny D's Thursday evening hosted
   poetry readings,
at which I read some work a number of times.
                    Music all kinds—
salsa, calypso, ragtime, R & B, jazz, Top 40, bluegrass
   & honky tonk,
& Friday Happy Hour was now the exclusive of Wally's Swing World
   & its dance scene,
even the pre-teen kid bands got to play on the open mike early evenings.
Celebrations & birthday parties, daytime dance & yoga classes,
   I myself offered education—
my Mythos of Santa Cruz talk I presented October 10th of '06.

    The E3 fostered community, it did,
& Wes, a jazz musician himself,
played in various bands & was a teacher of music to the young
for some 11 years already—how he wanted to inspire & was indeed
an inspiration & wanted so much that the E3 be known as a
social arts center for the community—
          But, you know, many,
as the grapevine had it, got the additional "Wes experience" too—
Oh, he could often be not quite level & straight with you,
he was seemingly so often distant, not quite present,
narcissistically aloof you would say at times, as if he harbored
  a private conceit of his own—
He would often make his point with impatient condescension.
Seemed he held himself, as the city claimed, above the law,
or so, as the story goes, despite his attempts to correct it,
  & however so many of us supporters came forward
    & made our plea to keep the E3 open.

          I remember
how Wes would suddenly appear & pace about on the floor
self-absorbed, playin' his clarinet in the pauses of the evening,
listening to the promptings of another, distant drummer.

       As it played out,
after Wes & friends made their case that day
in the chambers of the city council—but a line
he had already crossed & was too late to step back from—,
the E3 he was ordered to close & so Wes thumbed his nose
  at Santa Cruz,
overnight informing everyone he was planning
  come August
    a new cruise ship career up in Alaska...

      And it was here at the E3
I performed for the first time publicly
backed up by the keyboards & singing ambient tones
of the musical duo *Spirit Whisperers*,

               it was here, later that October '06
—another Thread woven into a much greater Story—
—it was Tuesday, October 24—
    that I debuted

         the Vision of Psyche

February 2008

Hula Hula

Every Sunday evening at the approach of the sunset hour,
it's been four years on, a gal she tells me, they gather here,
    out on the lawn,
in open view of the Sun going down, just beside
    the Cruzin' Surfing Museum,
            here, at Lighthouse Point—
HULA HULA—
Well, look, a whole colorful medley of hula hoops lean
against the red brick
         of the museum—
Like, it's understood you or anyone can grab one
& do the hula hula yourself, whatever your ability,
whatever your skill, however you wanna twirl & jig—
For sure, there are some real hoopie masters out here.
This evening, two guys names of Clay & Little John
have set up a table & DJ mixer & got the speakers out,
they're gonna crank up a rave of music too…

Each week, of course, it's different, it's whatever happens,
it's, like, spontaneous & extemporaneous, it's a sort'a sense of community,
    for those who regularly show up—
somethin' called fun, you know, for those who really get into it—

Oh, you can guess alright who's here—
The so many young, hippie-ish & gypsy-esque Santa Cruzans, of course,
their families & other kids who happen to show up, all kinds'a persons
are showin' up & standin' around, all kinds'a persons are hooping
with obviously practiced hips & legs & arms & shoulders & necks…
Oh, I know her—& there's the kid & dad,
& some guy is hula hoopin', managing to hold a leash to his dog,
& some bearded guy in a purple spiked cap & cosmic tie-dye T
was jugglin', like, those bowling pins a bit ago, now he's balancing
on a fingertip way above his head two bonded hoops—
oh, he *is* good at this, he's been at it, as you can see…

And people constant are walkin' by & stand about & watch.
And bicyclists ride up & slow their wheels way down & watch.

And a guitar player is solitarily strummin' round in front
    of the museum.
And waves come rollin' in all around Lighthouse Point.
And dark figures of surfers you see out in the sunset silvery water.
And there're three doin' an all feet-up-in-the-air group acrobatic trick.
And now the juggling staffs are brought out & guys are twirlin'.
And strange freaky clouds, like, hula hula way above us.
And the music keeps hula hoopin' all around us…

    It is dusk & the Full Moon
    should be rising
      soon…

And the bright candy color-lit hoops are brought out
& they're now twirlin'—these fast pulsin' circles are spinnin'
    & whirlin' of color—
And the mouths open & go

    WHOOO—! WHOOO—!

   AYA YAA YAA—! AYA YAA YAA—!

On evenings of warmer weather
—there's a chill comes in the air now—
the fire dancers really put on a show…

And the turned on beam of the lighthouse
is now goin' round & round pulsin' its light above all this
spinnin' & twirlin' & whirlin' & hula hoopin'…
everything is like music spinnin' & twirlin' & whirlin'—

    HULA! HULA!

And the Full Moon so big & so orange suddenly appears
in the break of cloud over distant waters of Monterey

   & joins in…

April 2011

Luminescence: a Spa
& *Kava Bar*

Luminescence, yes,
I suppose
you would say,
it is what starts to happen,
once
you start sippin' on,
sip...sip...
the kava kava
she serves here.
—Lizzie gets her kava
    from Hawaii,
            she says.

I'm sittin' at the round wood table,
the warm red-stain wood table,
with magazines & books & placemats all over,
a decorative big wood serving bowl & dipping cups
    & miscellanea,
& Rhonda's sittin' in one of the cushioned chairs,
we're talkin' with Lizzie & a regular guy here Peter
    who's talkin'—
The mouth gets numb drinkin' kava,
the mind—ahhh, that relaxing sort'a buzz,
you find yourself wanting to share, wanting to open up,
gettin' all warm & fuzzy like—
            They say
it's the social gathering drink
    of Hawaii & Polynesia—
it's like, that's the way it gets—
a little scintillating,
a little illuminating,
luminescent, I would say,
light essence going round—yes—
How about lumina luminescence?
O flash & flash—

All aglow, you know?
Even the parrots in their cage
just outside the inviting open door
squawking & whistling & mimicking,
laughing & sort'a purring
agree with us…
      & such
soft cushioned chairs,
soft carpeting & rugs
& pillows—
      Wow,
this is nice
   —gotta bring friends,
let's all drink kava kava…

Lizzie sits at her small wood altar of a counter,
her elixir mixing counter is against the wall,
just under the big stretched world turtle tapestry
  on the wall,
we're all in this mellow conversational flow,
like, this is the ritual scene, isn't it,
this is what it's like,
sip…sip…

blissed out….

13140 Highway 9, Boulder Creek
September 17, 2011

The Rave

                Was an evening of
      The Human Experience—
       "Broken Open," an album release—
And so I enter the experience,
& so many others are lining up, coming in,
     to enter the experience—
                       I drift in,
in the drift of more coming in,
into the gathering momentum of motion,
     the building up
             of an ambient trance
   of a unified motion—

No tables set out here tonight,
           no one is sitting,
      lights down low,
          but are dancing or standing, *so many*—
a bobbing head globular sea of bodies,
       it is *Be*-ing time,
               the beat the beat,
    it's a slinking between
       the interstices of bodies,
a wave of hands pointing into the air,
          arms all snaky,
   legs prancing like creatures…
             The Experience pulls you in,
   grooving to deep bass   a low low bass beat,
drums…drum drum…snap snap of snare drums,
electric haunting primal slow beat bowel rhythm…
            a woman is singing…
                 & above the stage
a computer generating graphic projecting screen,
     Tree of Life living unfolding geometry
  modulating, variating, expanding,
          fractal cell mitosis
  splitting, opening, pulsing,

                              in the waves of
         the slow cobra swaying bodies,
                   women sparkly glitter eyes,
           cheeks smile, show off iridescence,
                 fake fur boas, scarves, head scarves,
                           dreadlocks,
          tight clinging pants,
                         quite tight short skirts,
                bare long legs,
                              stockings such colors,
                    & those trans-dressed,
          reefer sweet smells
                        wafting,
& the hula hoops come out,
                       lights begin twirling,
& intricate-layered
                 wood-crafted
                               mandalas
         are on display,
& mounted light mandalas are pulsing pulsing…
A live painting artist, watch brush work—
                 a figure has taken form,
cultural icon portraits
                    in a row…
               the beat keeps / sustains
& DJ *The Human Experience*
    picks up & plays live to his tracks
        different
                 instruments,
                       so many *transitions*—
    slow slow
         slowed way down down motion,
deep tubular wood chimes
    pound
           pound the beat,
                    sounding down through
          cavernous places,
                        thump thump,
            the beat picks up picks up,

    suddenly are flutes on steroids,
          maracas, xylophone,
     intersecting humans hugging,
  & the self-absorption of many,
       swaying swaying…
Lotta beer goin' down,
cacao drinks…in dispensers…cups of neuro activation—
   gulping down fast neuron blasts,
       more hula hoops twirling
           twirling twirling,
      a lotta serious hula hooping,
   the back room all an open floor,
light lit colors twirling twirling
       gymnastic practiced indeed…
& at the main room bar all those sittin' & talkin',
   meeting friends…

    & it's gettin' late,
  after midnight…
      time for the poet
 to enter
     another dreamtime…

Did you experience?
Are you experienced?

The Human Experience

  did rave

  on such

  a night

Don Quixote's (now Felton Music Hall)
6275 Highway 9, Felton
February 23, 2017

VII

I am doing what a poet is supposed to do,
    he said—
I am out here, on the streets, hittin' the pavement,
immersed in my place, observing & assimilating with all
    my senses,
allowing the *Mythos* of this place, as he said, to live
    through me
        —oh, he did understand—,
that Mythos might with a poet's voice speak,
with such a Voice as it would voice

    this place

April 1, 2011
Santa Cruz
First Friday Art Walk
"he said" is Dennis Holt

They're Dude'n It

It's one of those crazy spinnin' summer fog cookin' nights
    here on Pacific Ave,
streams of persons just jammin', cruz'n, boppin' along,
meetin', hangin' out, congregatin', guitars playin', music all kinds
    like smoke in the air,
like it's the place to be for dudes & chicks like pourin' in thick
    & hot,
and the dudes are like dudes just dude'n it,
        they're dude'n it all over the place—

Hey dude, what dude'n are you dude'n?

Well, I'm tryin' to dude up this slick chick here, see?
Like I'm the dude who dudes the thing,
I dude it right—

        Yeah, she likes this dude.
Like, dude, you got it,
        just keep dude'n
whatever you're dude'n…

        What a dude, dude.

Hey, dude, what's happenin'?

And so it goes on this endless crazy spinnin' cruz'n night…

June 2000
from *The Multi Guy on Pacific Ave*

```
Tim, the bubble man,
          stands
                    on Front Street,
fine tuning his bubble machine—


             It's nine o'clock sharp
& the crowd-going are eager,
                              they'll pounce
              on just about anything.
And a crazy twirling wheel & fan contraption
                     is ready
              to spew
     a blizzard
                    of umpteen soap dreams
              into the night—


Cars mow them down
                    as they stream across
         a hurried indifference
                         to somewhere
              or another,
     & people passing
                    reach at them
              & pop,
                    hands pop
                         & pop.


His bubbles perish
                    by the thousands,
         yet streams
                    of thousands more
     sail for a ways
                    through the air.


         Odd spectacle,
bubbles continuously set free
         from a leggy machine—
```

301

Why he does it,
$\qquad$ every night?

Tim puffs on his pipe.

late 1980s

The Gique of Bubbles
for Michael

And now, years later,
           another bubblemaker
—calls himself the Bubble Gique—
stands downtown at his favorite spot
            corner of Pacific & Walnut
      on people-promenading weekend evenings
in his black tee & black beret,
         a black 5-gallon bucket
                on the curb cement
filled with enough soapy solution
        for hours
           of entertainment-making/
keep them coming attention-getting—
With two long stripped down twigs,
          a long, long shoe lace loop
                  attached,
  which into the bucket he dips
he slowly, skillfully, waves
              like choreographed wands
      producing huge moment-to-moment
           shifting
    amorphous shapes
that float away
          like transparent slow-motion
                  asteroid rock
  that instantly collapse to droplets
            or hit cars
        or slowly come at you,
their surfaces iridescent hypnotic-gleaming
                suddenly encompassing
    your whole vision.

People gather round in fascination,
             who knows what young girls imagine;
                 dollars are slipped
                 into a small white bucket—
& you step away before an asteroid makes impact.

1998

Magic Man/Magic Geeks
for Tom Connors

He sets up a little green satin-draped
magician's table
    under the bright light entrance of
    the well-known
           GAP
      (after closing)
& pulls in cruisin' passersby
      by hooks of flattery
       & sheer ingenious audacity—
Tom, totally into his role,
with yellow silk scarf wrapped gypsy-style
              round his head
       & yellow silk neck scarf,
  a glittery paisley felt vest
      & china blue black-trim silk jacket,
rolls out a continuous patter,
              his words
       juggled
    as fast as
       his conjurer's
            presti-
                digi-
                   tations.

      A woman comes up
      & says
      he tweaks kids—
        & their parents too—
As he does now
     with a kid & his dad—

You see on the table two red balls,
Ivan & Maria.

Pick one. Ivan or Maria.
Maria it is.
She sits in the palm of my hand.
Okay, now pay attention.
I'm putting Ivan in my pocket.
That makes how many balls in this hand?

         —One

No, two. See—

  There's surprise in faces.

Now let's try again.
I'm putting two in my pocket.
How many now in this hand?

         —Two

No, three.

     And amazingly *there are* three—
     Something magic is definitely afoot.

See, you're not paying attention.
Let's do it one last time.
Three go in my pocket.
Now how many balls in this hand?

  The puzzled kid
    & his perplexed dad
      don't know what to answer.

Now, look, it's a silver dollar.
Here— You want it?

And Tom extends his hand to give it
and the kid's hand is there
      to receive it,
  but comes up empty.

  —It was just there a second ago!

  Oh, there's no business like show business,
Tom says,
    as a few dollars
     —for real—
      go flyin' into a hat.

Suddenly, an old acquaintance
  —he'd been standing in front of us
    for sometime—
      calls out my name;
it's Rob, an engineering tech who used to work
  where I worked—
Like, we begin talkin' to catch up on things,
when, the next moment, the Friday night parade now brings—
    Lloyd & Jodell happen by
       & they start talkin'
     this cyber talk
    with Rob,
     like, they're totally into it—

As a semicircle of people
    gather once again round Tom,
  Jodell & Lloyd & Rob
      juggle
     visions of
    3-D multi-media tools machines
& digital sound processing & multi-tasking
& object-oriented & virtual sound programming
& Jodell aims next on getting a Next cube
     & Next dimension board
& Rob then brings out
     his palmtop computer
—sits in the palm of his hand with magic pen,
    makes icons appear & disappear—,
can connect with the Internet
     & digital cameras,

& they RAM & ROM & conjure all the ramifications
of fast number
    presti-
      digi-
        tations.

      And Jodell & Lloyd
    are going to set up
   their virtual reality console
  & pull in people
      cruisin' the Net
 & offer them verisimilitudes
that require
  a certain
    paying
  of attention—

I turn & see Tom wowing a crowd
with old-fashioned rope tricks.

Oh, there's no business like show business...

1998

He's on a Mission Caravan

Is Pacific Ave alive & energized tonight!
Wow are people the capillaries of life in the flow
up & down the Ave this beautifully mild Friday
    of a June twilight—
And listen to that constant boom of song—!
You could hear it blastin' all the way from here
on Front St. (where Rhonda & I had been sippin'
    chocolate at Mutari Chocolate),
& now has us walkin' toward, pulled in, to the Ave—
It's a vortex of a big poundin' blast of song,
    pullin' people in—
It's the giant of a moving caravan peace show,
parked right alongside the curb front of
    the bar Motiv.
It's the *I'm on a mission caravan on wheels*—
Yes, it's the Santa Cruz Peace Train…

                You've undoubtedly
seen it before on the streets of The Cruz,
you've heard its speaker loud blastin' cruz'n along
on the streets of The Cruz…even up through
the San Lorenzo Valley…was recently in Felton…
Two big tall van trailers hitched to a Ford F-350
    XL Super Duty.
It's the Follow Your Heart Action Network,
    masterminded by Curtis Reliford,
an inspired man with compassion for the needy—
And he's grand waving the American flag up there,
on top the second of the performance vans—
Eight of 'em are dancing / in motion on top
    of a travelling stage up there—
One is swayin' to the beat with a Peace spelled-out sign.
And messages are plastered all over this caravan:

LIFE IS WHAT YOU MAKE IT
HELP ME SHOW LOVE TO THE HOPI
RESERVATION! THIS IS MY 5TH TRIP
GOING THERE TO GIVE AWAY FOOD, CLOTHES
AND BUILDING MATERIALS
I NEED GAS TO GET THERE
EMPATHY   KINDNESS

    PEACE

JOIN US ON A JOURNEY
OF KINDNESS
(with images of Martin Luther King & Gandhi)

BE THE CHANGE
YOU WISH TO SEE
IN THE WORLD

THOU   STOP
SHALL   KILLING
NOT KILL

We face a moral crisis as a country and as a people.
Those who do nothing are inviting shame as well as violence.

JOIN US ON A JOURNEY OF KINDNESS
PEACE   PEACE

The soulful music vocals are pumpin' singin' loud,
& people on the sidewalk both sides the Ave are groovin' it—
Moment to moment, spontaneous dancing is breakin' out,
young women walkin' along start skippin' & dancin' along…
And others stand around, smart phone photos taken…
And standin' next the Peace Train at a table
is expo MC & singer of his own band Robert Perala,
    with whom we chat a bit.

Oh, yes, the loud *good* vibes of peace & compassion,
    of kindness,
reverberate in waves up & down the Ave.

It's another spontaneous
INSPIRED EVENING
for all
on Pacific Ave.

June 8, 2018

The Street Poet

           Mark, the Street Poet,
been doin' his thing on Pacific Ave
on & off for years,
    he said,
& that was about almost all he said
after I came up & introduced myself,
    The Multi Guy—
                That's
after seeing his ragged cardboard sign
    'bout him
      bein' a street poet legend.
And almost immediately,
    he put up a wall,
wouldn't at succeeding opportunities
    even cast his eyes on me,
        'specially when I performed
    just down the Ave a ways.
He avoided me like something serious.
I suppose he considered the Ave
    his territory,
      like, this was
               his gig.

        Oh,
      he also
    did make a point
      of saying
        he was
    a *genuine* street poet,
I suppose to distinguish himself
from those of us who, in his eyes,
    apparently aren't—
And I suppose, you would have to say,
    it was true,
if indeed he made his living this way.

Considering what I saw,
        what he had to offer
—a few meager lookin',
           typewritten poems,
none currently available to actually sell
    —a donation rather
      was what
           he was after,
& then he'd read a poem—,
      while presenting a persona like a wall—,
it must be a life fairly difficult,
to make a living this way.

          —Oh,
as he also
      did say
          it was.

(June 2000)
January 2001

Brandon: The Ringleader

                      Was a scene perhaps
no different, in essence, than what
might have taken place in ancient Athens—

                                  Those were the years
of sittin' round the tables outside the original Pergolesi,
its enclosed, wood-backed benches, a double terrace,
bird perched alongside a cobblestone walkway,
directly behind Bookshop Santa Cruz, its rear door opened to—
For some years, day after day, in the late 1970s,
turn of the 80s, the young, student intellectuals would gather here,
daily sippin' their coffee & espressos, smokin' their Camels
    & Galoises,
readin' with ravenous, nonstop appetite all the avant-garde
among thinkers & writers & literary critics, especially those
who were now coming into prominence as Postmodernists,
which meant primarily those of the European
    intelligentsia.
                                  And the ringleader
amongst this circle of philosophical decadence,
in this contemporary agon of no holds barred,
was reveling in it all, brilliant, mental-muscled Brandon,
a somewhat older, a sometimes UC student,
always showing up in his trademark disheveled,
just-gotten-up look, after typically sleepin'
another night on someone's living room sofa—
Uncombed, tangled hair, a rugged Bukowski face,
his dark Scorpio eyes could pierce & rivet you, holding you
suspect for your every word; a cynical, ironic, demeanor,
but always, he meant only to playfully mock…

                    Brandon, one quickly recognized,
had an impressively verbal intellect—
Effortless monologue discourse he could carry on at length;

he could improvise dissertation quality critiques zeroed in on
   just about anything,
                        or anyone who happened along
& whose curiosity was drawn into their cerebral baited trap—
Wielding his long, multiple-clause, mercilessly mesmerizing,
serpentine twisting, whip-like, biting sentences that could unmask
any pretension, expose any naiveté, deflate any arrogant pose,
shame any unconscious fascist attitude into revealing itself,
spinnin' language faster than even the devil, if you could follow…
Everything, to him, was text, which he took the greatest pleasure
especially in exposing the Freudian or capitalist underbelly of,
or picking apart into endlessly clever word play—
He saw consumerist hooks in every sunset,
in every inviting country road, codifications he saw
for the latest automobile ads—
                        He'd take a whiff
of commercial-free exhaust off an idling car—
   Aaaa, he would snicker,
   the real smell of capitalism—

                He could bring a woman
almost to tears after she casually remarked
she had just come from a shower;
how self-conscious—exposed—he made her feel,
calling her out on her fresh-smelling, bourgeois,
   unmediated, innocence.
And he was not to be cornered into any simplification,
as if his character were merely that of a brainy bully,
it was that he wanted an uncompromising, Saturnine honesty,
keeping true, as he claimed, to a knife's-edge,
intellectual conscience.

                      To one side of him
often sat media student, sidekick Ken, & on the other,
precocious, even some years younger, Scott,
who shared bouts in this daily gathering of harmless sophistry,

despite, perhaps, a previous night's debauch of drinking & drugs
—& none of that seemed to faze Brandon a bit—,
marshalling to the marvel of all who listened in
the social, cultural, psychoanalytical, philosophical critiques
offered by contemporary Marxists & Freudians,
by old Nietzsche, without saying, & Benjamin, Adorno,
Horkheimer, Habermas, Barthes, Foucault, Lacan,
Deleuze, Baudrillard, Lyotard, & the darling
     of them all—
                Derrida...

             Remarkably,
Brandon was also able to parody
the language of the old Romantics, mystics, theologians,
of Jungians & Heideggerians, of occultists & New Agers,
of all metaphysicians who were to them laughable obscurantists,
which is to say, all who still engaged in the great cop-outs
     of intuition, feeling & visions,
all who incredibly still spoke of some transcendent Other
or Greater Reality, of some abstract spiritual or archetypal realm,
like they couldn't believe their ears hearin' Ral speak
     of his mythic visions,
this throwback anachronistic poet to the 19th Century,
livin' smack in a Postmodern, decadent, late capitalist,
consumerist culture that had been deconstructed
of ageless Tradition's metaphysical superstructure—
They always chuckled at artists' old Romantic pretensions,
any talk of mythopoesis, any hint of invoking dead
     Gods & Goddesses—
             Like, what?
                      Brandon
always wondered when Ral would disabuse himself
of his autistic delusion of some inside track to Divinity,
still referencing grandiose transcendental signifiers
that had propped up the cultural illusions of the past...

                These were the days
when he would prod the poet,
    Ral, when are you going to introduce us
    to one of your beautiful Goddesses in person
    so that we might behold such a verisimilitude in mortal form
    who valorizes your archaic mythical poet's dream
    of breathing life again into an original language...

2012/2016

George

                Oh, there's George,
in his tan corduroy sports jacket
& throwback Sixties bell bottom pants,
wearin' his trademark pointed black hat
    —been wearin' it for years—,
& stringy, pointed, red beard, lookin' like an overgrown
    lost elf.
He's been out cruz'n on these streets a long time now,
always seemin' to be engaged in workin' out
    the kinks of his own private world
            —never with anyone, it seems—
    always, like, trippin' along by himself—
Though he used to visit us years ago,
that is, the once upon a time short life I had with Vivian,
when we hosted these astrology potluck get-togethers,
fillin' our living room with all of our local astrologers
    & all their big, star-defined egos.
                        But George—
now he certainly was different, was quite the oddball,
somehow I was able to him draw out; the others largely
    ignored him.
Who today would even know he was a damn good astrologer
    himself,
even quirky enough as to have the generational planets
Uranus, Neptune & Pluto,
                their positions,
            year by year,
        by degree,
     memorized—
A walking ephemeris, he was.

And when he gets talkin' real animated-like,
his hands do this jerky thing,
    as if
          they're helpin' him get

    all the stutterin'

       the stutterin'

    all the stutterin' words

          to come out.

December 2000

Eucalyptus Man
>*for Jim Short*

       Now Jim
     has an ongoing affair
with the most unusual
        among trees—
     He goes up
  to the Arboretum
       at UCSC
   to meet them
     for a tryst—
(They tout more species
  of eucalyptus,
    he says,
   than anywhere
      outside of Australia.)
He says
  he communes
     with the mysterious eucalyptus,
  he loves to be
    in their presence,
says he feels points of energetic release
       when he approaches them,
the tips of each branch,
    as he brushes them
      electric to the flesh—

People, he says,
   are actually afraid
      of the eucalyptus,
  that's if
   you can get them
      to even think about it
   (something of a strange notion of his,
       you must admit)
  for the eucalyptuses are such, he says,

                              hyperactive trees,
        but you need to become
                                   very still
            to truly experience them—

                        And so he stretches out
            beneath the stately ones there
                        within the boundary
                                of the Arboretum,
             he stretches out
                        beneath the ones
                                    that rise proud,
        fills his nostrils
                    with the sweat
                                of their oozing leaves,
            watches
                    as the leaves follow
                                the path of the Sun,
                hears them
                        crackle & pop
                                    as they turn—

                        He loses all sense of time
                in his reverie of the eucalyptus
            on the hottest of days—
        Rangers were about to look
                        for him
            when they were about to close the gate
        (they had counted how many
                                had gone in,
            came up one short
                        who had not yet come out.)

                                You know, he says,
                    you can actually hear
                a eucalyptus growing—

                In fact,
   among their great diversity, he says,
               —fourteen hundred species,
                           according to him,
         from scraggly vines
                  creeping around rocks
                              of high altitudes
          to giant mammoths
                    you can drive
                              a truck through—
      are found the fastest growing of trees
               —one clocked in at 36 feet in 12 months,
                  he says—
& the longest of leaves
                  —at 3 3/4 foot,
      with the greatest spectrum of colors
                  —ghostly white & lunar silver,
                all the varieties of gray,
                     & black, blue, yellow, gold,
                          red, pink & purple,
                including of course
                           all the commonly known greens—,
 & among them are the largest of flowers
                            —at 7–8 inches,
       & he says
                 they're among the tallest of trees,
                       despite all the focus
            on the redwood
                        & others;
 & one among their kind, he says,
                         has the densest of wood
         —takes a diamond saw to cut it—
                  —iron bark they call it—;
        & they are also, he says,
                          the most aggressive of trees—
                If they choose,
      they can eliminate

                    other living things
                                    around them
            (they've learned over time
                            sundry sly techniques)
                —even the branches
                            practice a kind of
            survival-of-the-fittest;
& they are impossible to kill, he insists,
            unless, that is,
                            you happen to know
            the location of their heart.
                    (But that is a secret.)
Those know who have tried—
                Cut 'em down,
            burn 'em,
& they come back with a vengeance.

                So unusual
                    is the mysterious eucalyptus,
    ever curious Jim
                        has all these questions
                about them
                            that, as he says,
                to this day
                            go unanswered.
        And though
                    they might intimidate people
        (as he claims)
                        he loves their intimacy—
                Stand beneath them awhile
        & you might get a sense
                        of just what he means.

1998

Café Fast One

            He tried to pull a fast one on me—
I was waitin' for my iced cappuccino
    & Aaron, barista behind the counter
                at The Ugly Mug,
wearin' green baggy pants,
        a heavy chain hangin'
                from front to back pocket,
    blue casual t-shirt,
    blue backwards baseball cap
                perched
      on a buzz cut,
  a ring in his nose,
        various sized rings danglin'
                from both ears
—I saw him once
        barrel his skateboard
                down the café floor—

                I'm standin' there
& he's tellin' me how he at one time
        taught
            at a school
    in New York City
                back in the 70s
  —and here it's '98—

"Oh, I'm older than I look—"
he said,
        straight-faced,
as casual as could be.

The Ugly Mug, Soquel
1998

Kelsey

She swung open the double doors of The Mug
sporting this short-cropped, orangish, boyish hair
        —like androgynous, you know,
   she's, like, eccentric, you know—
one day in oversized welder's coveralls,
another day, crowned enigmatically in a bridal veil—
so she steps inside with this guy,
as if a prize she had just won,
    —oh, he's been around,
        they've been hangin' together—
& so they stood there, just inside the door,
& she boldly announced aloud to all present,
   Hello, everyone—
   I want to introduce Patrick.
   He's a really nice guy.
   I like him a lot.
   And I can't wait to take him home.

Suddenly, there's clapping throughout the place,
immediately upon which she whisked him
        —who didn't say a word,
   he just stood there, modest-like & smiled—,
back out the door.

By the way, she's an employee here.

The Ugly Mug, Soquel
December 2000

To Rose

Rose is a rose is a
maybe not a rose?
Is she maybe not a rose?
Is she not still, though, maybe a rose?
Is she not maybe not a rose?
Is she not maybe not not a rose?
Is she maybe not?
Is not still perhaps maybe?
Or is maybe perhaps not?
Is she maybe somewhat a rose?
Is Rose not a rose if not somewhat a rose?
Is she not somewhat maybe a rose?
Is she not not somewhat maybe a rose?
She is, not is not, Rose is perhaps a kind'a rose.
But is Rose in a multitude of roses
a white rose? a black rose?
a red rose? a purple rose?
Is Rose a pink rose?
Is Rose a rose? Or not?
If not, then what is what?
Even a rose among thorns is still a rose.

Is she?
Is she not?
Is Rose a rose?
How many Roses are there?
Is there a Rose of all roses?

You decide

July 2003

Shelton

Has that sharp New York bark,
& he put on this green Ché Guevara bandanna
    someone had given him
with holes he slaughtered in it for eyes as a mask
    to show off something of his past—
White beard, white fringed bald top, friendly, sociable, cranky guy,
always wanting a high five, used to be a union organizer,
said he knew quite a few rock stars in his time.

        And there's this woman in pink
sitting with her laptop computer
utterly absorbed in it at one of the other further away café tables,
& Shelton turned from the couple friends he happened to be with
& looked across half the room & loudly addressed her,
she being the only obvious person in that direction,
    Are you a computer geek?

No, but my boyfriend is.

What are you doing?

She says something I cannot hear,
but Shelton barks back what I certainly do hear,
    You're playing games? Playing games?
    Why aren't you out there protesting
        against the rich?
And she says something about the rich, maybe it was
she had a bit of money herself & wouldn't imagine
    doing such a thing,
& Shelton barks out even louder,
    Get the troops out of Iraq!
    Get the troops out of Iraq!

A Jew from New York
he always loudly, proudly, says.

The Ugly Mug, Soquel
July 2004

Deep South Voice

Always you find him sittin' here on Pacific Ave,
always playin' his leisurely slow-strum guitar,
singin' his always leisurely Deep South blues,
    his often mournful song—
You see him—always the head turned down.
It's the straw hat always hides the face
    —and his head turned down.
But that deep deep soulful voice of his
    carries far,
always gives him away,
from even blocks away.

Pacific Avenue
August 2004

The Great Morgani

    Julio, The Great Morgani—
Could you ever at this point surpass yourself?
You sit in the alcove of Dell Williams tonight,
an accomplished accordionist, yes, indeed you are—
You've performed for hundreds transfixed by you
    along the Avenue;
        & it's been quite a number of years now—
Oh, I remember you back then, when you first started
    to make your local impression.
                But, you do know,
    it is not the music itself you play,
however good you are, & however extensive your repertoire—
It is *the other* that has gotten you your recognition,
it is *the other* you consistently embody
    that it might reveal
              its play.

    Julio, tonight,
as only a one night's example, you call something out of us
that almost—disturbs us? unnerves us? is sort'a creepy?
brings out something we cannot quite cozy up to?
                You play for us some tune,
sitting in the alcove as if on your own stage,
a bright orange nun's habit you wear,
a white white face you wear with painted teeth-wide grin,
these heavy black-shadowed eyes like dark dark sunglasses,
    your black gloves moving
              as if disembodied
        to the slow rocking of your accordion—
People, I can tell, almost don't know
what to think of you tonight, Julio,
    you are that bizarre tonight,
              but, then,
perhaps no more bizarre than on
    a hundred other nights.

You are The Amazing Great Morgani of the Avenue—
Performance artist of costume one-of-a-kind
    extraordinaire—
Behind the endlessly clever, ever-changing masks,
seems, though, a rather unassuming person you are—
Something *other* must live inside of you
that so convincingly demands to be
                                     outside.

Pacific Avenue
August 2004

Slow way down

It's one way to see a lot—slow down, *way down*.

    Back a couple of months
Robert said he got the idea
to start doin' this rather curious ritual down the sidewalk
 of the Ave—
Holding up an umbrella made of shiny milar,
covered all over with its jungle-color images of flowers & birds,
Robert, wearing his usual flowery shirt, white cap
 & white pants,
inches his way down the sidewalk of the Ave,
one very tiny of a slow motion, one very tiny step at a time—
One tiny step in front of the other, step by tiny step,
 as he smiles his smiley face.
      Step by tiny step,
   step by tiny step,
his reference of space & time must be utterly
on a different track to the river of humanity
 sweeping all around him—
People are like, in comparison, speeding past him.

Something over two hours it takes him
 to walk
   both sides the Ave—
In that time it's a whole lot he must see.

Pacific Avenue
August 2004

An Epiphany of Pink

Even the chilling fog of an August evening
    doesn't keep them away—
You see 'em all streamin' in to cruise the Ave—
It is the Vortex of The Cruz, you know,
    & it's summertime tourist season too,
        caught up as everyone you see here
                in the Vortex of The Cruz—
People flowing & flowing by, wave after wave flowing by,
those dressed as if for winter & those dressed despite the chill
    for what should be summer.

        It is an evening of gray upon gray...
& I spot—it had to be him,
he's acquired the reputation as the Umbrella Guy now,
no one else would be poising an umbrella over his shoulders
    and barely seemin' to be movin' at all—
But—it has been a while now since I've been on the Ave,
    because, like,
        what's this cross-dress, like, costume thing,
    or what?
        A skirt, pink tights?

            I approach him
& it all hits me, he's an epiphany of pink, he is—
I wouldn't have imagined it, but there he is, all dressed
    in feminine pink—
Pink tights, pink flowery skirt, one of these pink fluffy blouses,
    pink boa wrapped around shoulders,
pinkish-red lipstick, bright pink spotted cheeks & blush all over,
    a puffy pink hat & neat little pink purse,
        & of course—now it's a pink umbrella.
            And he's taking his tiny tiny steps
        & doesn't say a word,
he now maintains a strict silence, apparently,
you're not going to get a word out of him—

                    He stops & he'll smile
        & gives a tiny wave with his hand,
                                as he's doing now,
waving ever so slightly to a kid stopped with his mom,
    —they're a short distance away—,
& they all just stand there, smiling back & forth, a full minute seems
    before mom breaks the trance
        & tells her son *Okay, it's time to go*,
                    & so Umbrella Guy continues the tiny steps
            of his ritual,
continues in the swirling currents of the Vortex of The Cruz,
where there's quite a line, I see, goin' out the door of Pizza My Heart,
where, down by the big cement planter box front of New Leaf Market,
    next the Alfresco food kiosk,
there's a woman playin' guitar, another striking claves,
                        & a third standin' there, with them,
            & they are all singin',
                a sign leaning against the cement edge
    says
        Society for Artistic Freedom & Expression,
        & another sign they got
                        spelled as an acronym: SAFE.
They got a big pink candle burning, all kinds'a stuff piled around
    like a little makeshift altar.
                    Across the street, in front of GAP,
there's a group of four singin' some East Indian song,
sounding like out of the Krishna movement,
    I can't exactly tell.

                        And then,
wha'd'you know, as I'm about to leave the Ave,
there's a woman now I spot dressed in pink
    sittin' outside Kianti Pizza & Pasta bar,
wearin' a pink jacket, skirt with pink flowers,
    with a pink flower in her hair,
            talkin' on her cell phone,

& a moment later
she gets up to go into the restaurant—
You know, I spot pink shoes too.

                And then I look down the Ave
on such a gray upon gray of a foggy overcast evening
& I see pink the color of awnings on a building not far,
& pink the color of a building down a little further still,
    & there's another,
           & another—
Oh, I see pink showing up

                everywhere.

          And wouldn't you know,
I'm wearin' a pink pullover top.

Pacific Avenue
August 2005

Balloon Wizard Mark

You'll see him all the time on the Ave,
he's become quite the balloon wizard, Mark has,
like, he seems permanently to have established himself here—
He's the guy who used to do the puppet thing years back
    with a funky ol' cassette player playin',
                        which still does accompany him;
& he wears a color-striped vest over a sports number shirt,
    a stiff black derby on his head—
Does look like he could be your any Santa Cruz surfer, really.
His cart of all kinds'a balloon-making paraphernalia is parked close by,
& this tall, lookin'-like-a-candle, checkerboard pattern pillar
    is positioned
        in front of him—
               An air pump's inside,
& he's blowin' up these long sausage, of all kinds'a color, balloons
to twist into shape of whatever kids happening by with their parents
    want him to make.
             And while he's twistin' & twistin'
all these balloons together
    into all sorts'a animals, or whatever,
           he carries on his small talk patter—

                    Most remarkably,
he recently created a whole small scale, but still good-sized
    replica motorcycle
            —which I got to see firsthand—,
with its red bulging balloon fenders, a silvery chrome balloon body,
    even white-walled balloon tires,
& he has big photos propped up nearby to prove he did it
    for all who pass by—

        We exchanged a few words,
remembering times past on the Ave,

& he acknowledged my doin' my thing,
just as he was proud to be doin' his creative thing—
And I could tell, he's all heart to bring smiles
    to little girls & boys.

Pacific Avenue
November 2005

Lost Poets Salon
>*for Anita*

In what she calls her Rumi Gardens Anita conducts her Lost Poets salon—
And where in The Cruz might *this* be? It's the plant-extravagant patio
    outside the sliding glass door of The Bagelry.
See the showy white of calla lily, the nasturtium & morning glory?
They greet you as you walk up to & through a thick, ivy-matted,
woodwork lattice—an archway bringing you into Anita's poetry world.
And wouldn't the charmed soul see it this way, this jungle of green
    surrounding,
                  defining its own enclosed niche,
with little, white, scented flowers of jasmine, a lemon tree popping
    the giant of fruit,
with ivy flowing torrentially over the roof like a waterfall down the side
    of the building—
Poets gather here once a month, usually a handful at least,
sometimes a whole big circle of them gather round tables & take turns
    sharing their poems going round—
You find among them the modest, the sensitive, the thoughtful of poets,
    the dramatic & difficult of poets,
        the especially quirky among quirky poets,
            yes, the butterfly among poets,
    & the hawk,
               & the mother of poets among poets—

        It is Anita's glory, bringing them all together—
Oh, you would recognize her, those thick, narrow-lens glasses,
big eyes looking through her particularly narrow tunnel vision—
You have to appear just about smack in front of her for her to really
    see you;
        it's your identifying voice she typically hears first.
She shuffles along slowly, forward bent, has a big bright red lipstick smile,
big brooch clasping a sticking out girlie-like tuft of hair, her own voice
    like a warm, crackling fire,
                but beware—

It'll spark up wildly upon a word, or some misperceived impression
    she might have heard.
Her persistence year after year in bringing poets together here
but hints of a long life of dedication to the art—
Her heart must be made of poetry to have sprung
    such a garden
             to gather poets.

Oh, she feels as young as poetry ever is young.

The Bagelry, Cedar St.
December 2005

    And Alan "Sitar" Brown
you come to find out
also plays quite beautiful piano—
Walkin' along takin' in all the myriad of Avenue
  sights & sounds
of this wonderfully summery of summer evenings,
         Rhonda & I
happen to catch him out on the Ave
playin' his big wood, portable-on-wheels, piano,
parked on the sidewalk in front of the Hawaiian shop
  Kaleponi,
which is between the well-known Palomar Inn
  & Santa Cruz Coffee Roasting.
His famous sitar you could see laid across the front seat
of a shiny new VW van, its side door slid wide open,
parked behind him alongside the curb.
Looked like plenty of dollars were piling up
inside the clear plastic box on top the piano.
He played beautifully,
      that is, until
a police officer arrived & mentioned
  a complaint
      from an unspecified someone
    in an apartment above the street
for the noise,
    & makes Alan stop playing
what is obviously melodically beautiful music.
Even the officer, upon stepping up, said,
  It is lovely music, but...

      And a man name of Crow,
who with another were both hanging out
  with Alan,
hanging around out of the side of the van,
asked all these questions of the officer
about why Alan's music
  had to stop.

All these questions Crow asked,
all these questions Crow asked,
& sounded as if he never got
a satisfactory answer...

Pacific Avenue
July 1, 2006

Mr. TV

So it's Mr. TV set up on Pacific Avenue this evening—
He stands behind his busted out frame of a TV screen
that sits on top a tall, dark pink-draped sort'a stand.
He peeks out from glasses behind his virtual screen
in his gold-flecked jacket over a white shirt,
with a snappy bowtie & atop his head a yellow,
    sort'a cone-shaped hat,
& all kinds'a miniature props & dialogue script
    he's got on hand—
                      Does skits of Iraq—
I-rock, he says, producing a rock to make his point;
then urban jungle cops & thugs with toy patrol car
    & helicopter
—its sound he imitates as he flies it in—;
then a Howard Stern cut-out & Playboy model doll,
    he does some parody of;
                      & then Reality Street,
something about not making it on Sesame Street,
but somehow ending up in a sort'a prison
where, like, numbers are supposed to be recited—
Couldn't quite make that one out.
But you see how it all gets enacted
in this empty frame of a TV screen.
Calls his act the world's first organic television;
pay per view his intent, of course—
He pulls off his hat & tries to collect
from those watchin'
a dollar or two.

Pacific Avenue
August 2006

Calls Himself Nicho
for Dennis Holt

Wears a straw hat with a feather sticking out—
Hides the bald crown; white beard & moustache, wears glasses—
The former professor,
      as you will quickly discover.
Such warm, sensitive eyes, though, when the professor backs off
 & is silent a moment.
Always a guitar in its black cloth case strapped tight to his back,
 a leather bag on his shoulder,
you would most likely encounter him in his apparently favorite
burnt orange shirt, green over-shirt, always trekking along
 in the casual of sandals.
Once a word—any word—is spoken, you'll find out, is all it takes
& his former linguistic degree credentials spill out in a stream
 of detailed, meandering etymologies,
his barely restrainable loquacity unloading a library of years of study.
He can almost not stop. But he turns silent, eventually.
 Those eyes—
Intellectual eyes that suddenly turn downward & soft.

And let him play his Spanish guitar & sing these melodious
 Latin songs—
Be in for a surprise how beautifully these deep roots within him
 can sound,
why he calls himself
    Nicho.

September 2006

Firefly Fridays
for Brian Morrissey

     These little poetry scenes,
they're always poppin' up
& happenin' somewhere, you know,
you try to remember 'em all, over the years,
    you might as well forget it—
To keep the scene going, though, is the trick, that's the secret,
perhaps you might someday even hear about one
    that's become something legendary—
Like, say, here, at the Firefly Café, Brian's been keepin' it going
    for 2 ½ years now.
The café itself has its own little niche in the Wired Wash,
    a laundromat, imagine, of all places.
Every Friday evening you got the poets comin' in
& this little audience sittin' around the blue & green painted tables,
& you got some standin' back & leanin' on the serving counter
    wrapped round behind—
Like at all these poetry scenes, you sign up & take your turn to read,
everyone is given a chance, like, anyone can come up to the mike
    & share somethin' out of poesy's soul—
You stand against the yellow wall goin' up to a high black ceiling,
a warm, soft glow there the 5-flowered stand-up light gives
    that really makes it a dreamy sort'a scene—
Above the sofa along the window you see the poets reading,
    from a whole other reflected angle,
        their silhouettes you see—
It is as if out of some dream you might have had
    of some such little poetry scene.   And you will hear
some gems of poetry here, yes, gems & silver & gold,
you will hear veins exposed of rich soul lore out of the matrix
    of life's dark matter.   Thankfully
the living, spoken, embodied, sweet Muse-sounding word
still finds its niches in this poetically impoverished world.

Wired Wash / Firefly Café, Laurel St., Santa Cruz
November 2006

A Hit'a Words
upon attending recent poetry readings

Man, it's that hit'a words you get,
like, I'm sure you'll know what I mean,
you're hit by somethin' that good,
    as good as it gets,
        as good as it ever gets,
            language is singin' to the max,
as powerful as words soundin' so beautiful
    can be—
                It's the connect
of connection, the bright flashin' of spoken electricity,
the conjunct of conjunction fusing extreme-ended
    poles of polarity,
        it's the contracted contraction
of comin' together unbridled, leapin' all over of energy,
the concise & super-excellent pop of syllable sound,
the unmistakable spirit quintessence that drugs
    don't got that power,
        not that blast of O for the soul—
Only the poet's voice got that power,
that sudden sweeping realization
    that this is, like, the real kick'a juice,
            'cause you know what it's got,
        the lightning bolt inside it,
gonna make you zigzag 'cross the sky,
spaces & places you see open between the words,
    between the sentences,
               such universes
    of meaning.
Oh, man, are you lit up with words,
your bein' is BEIN' this HERE & NOW—
I can see your eyes, man, you got hit
by somethin' that good.

December 1, 2006

Art Opening(s)

so many people, faces, voices
—wow, it's noisy this place—
    —so many, I get these glances,
      familiar faces—
        well, look at this—
cheeses, olives, meatballs—
    & bread—
O yes, wine back at the door
—how did I pass that up?—
    —& poured already too—
ah, nice—
      I'll take a glass—
        Thank you—
    & yes, let's do some
    olive oil tasting too—
this is the True Olive Connection store,
    after all—
        oh, &
          They got art
    up on the walls
        —look—,
She says.

        …Felix Kulpa I'm at
    & they got
crackers, celery & carrot sticks,
little tops of broccoli, some sort'a dipping sauce,
      mini-wraps—
    more cheeses—
  —& wine—
      & sparkling water—!
& there's, you know—
      Oh, hi! How are you?
    —talk, talk,
      yammer, yammer…

& who's that...?

*Just start
looking at the art,*
She says to me...

and there's—
she's familiar—vaguely familiar—
can't remember her name though—
sittin' there lookin' at me,
　　　　　　　this band's playin'
kind'a loud—couldn't talk anyway—
　　　(Museum of Art & History here
　　　　　in the big alcove)
& there's—
wow, must be 20 years ago or more—
　　　—we do the glance & glance—
some of the old Happy Hour Gang
still circulates, I see—

　　　& there's all that food outside the doors—
some pasta salad, mini-tacos,
　　　nuts, chips
　　　　　—wine at that table—

*Go upstairs
& start looking at the art,*
She says to me...

　　　across the alleyway...Artisans—
they got little slices of cake here,
wow, that frosting is sweet—
　　　little cups of wine—
　Oh, hi—
　　　　What are you up to...?

　　　Talk, talk,
yammer, yammer—

       & then—

    Just start
looking at the art—
She says to me.
(oh, *Her* voice I know)

Santa Cruz
First Friday Art Walk
May 6, 2011

Sheila's Outrage – Outreach

                      Taking me first
to one side—the left—of the gallery,
Sheila showed me & shared with me the stories
behind the various paintings she had done over the years
—literally almost all were portraits or figures.
A couple you would recognize as cultural icons
                      —two side by side of Mother Teresa,
with a letter displayed Sheila received signed by her,
in acknowledgement of the paintings,
& the Pablo Picasso above them is excellent—
                                Among the works
are also one or two well-known icons of the local Santa Cruz scene,
but obvious in so many of the others was the pervading eroticism,
    the explicit sensuousness,
a few quite explicit in open sexual theme—
                              Sheila's sensibility
brought out in paint like this was quite apparent then,
it was important that you saw it,
    because, *because*—
                          You really couldn't miss at first
as you walked into the gallery—how could you not see
the large, long-drawn-out, mock American flags
made of strips of bandages emanating from above the central
    raw wood staircase,
their shredded ends hung over beams high up near the high high ceiling,
two long shredded American flags soaked in the red of blood
    for the red stripes of our flag;
&, instead of stars, where the stars should be, white crosses you see,
all this as background to our two political party icons displayed—
One an elephant under which states *Elepantus vitio,*
    translating as *Corrupt elephant.*
The other a donkey under which states *Asinus sum,*
    translating as *I am an ass.*
                  As if that
were not enough to make impact,

you realize there is much more going on here,
    as you moved forward in time—
The radical departure of her newer work came,
    she said,
        after 9/11,
so radically a whole new & different direction her work took.

        Look, there, on the right wall,
how could you not see *those portraits*,
those hauntingly wicked wicked portraits lookin' back at you—
You look long enough, you stare long enough, & they start to make
    a disturbance in your soul,
this is as political as art can get, it can't get blunter than this—

The September 11, 2001 cross on gray painting began the series,
& bam bam bam these portraits of accursedness hit you
    & do they hit you—
All the Bush—aka King George—White House people are there,
George W himself, of course, in two or three of the works,
& Colin Powell, Dicki Cheney, Condi Rice,
Karl Rove—Bush's Brain is lettered in the middle
    of the huge forehead—,
        Rummi Rumsfeld
—Abu Ghraib spelled out on his prominent blue collar—,
Wolfi (hiding in one of the works) & Ashcroft,
& there's also the scapegoat of this terrible disaster of current war,
    Saddam Hussein,
& further down, there is yet another you see of Ariel Sharon
    & Yassar Arafat,
        upside down to each other,
            flipping each other off—
Oh, when we stood here, Sheila did have something to say
    about all of them.
        Radical departure, for sure—
Sheila said she was shaken out of the American Dream,
turned nightmare since 9/11 & the Iraq War,
she tapped in herself such outrage, that she could produce
    such portraits—

                    They look as if they were done
by someone much much younger, in fact,
the collage high impact background to each portrait
hitting you with their images of violence & death, words venting,
words spattered of lies, conspiracy & the playing cards of Condi's
    machinations,
the raw words painted on like some in-your-face punker style,
how they hit you, scream out at you, they are so disquieting,
    so disquieting.

                        And then,
how could you miss the sculptures by Eike,
    her husband,
on raised pedestals with their own provocative social/political themes—
You see one a slew of these polished gray stone elephants
humping over white donkeys—
                        And Eike
stood at the small platform up at the turn of the steps
of the central staircase; before a stand he stood,
a little reading light he had, a microphone,
& delivered a moving statement about America
    since 9/11,
                    about freedom & democracy
he was so compelled to speak out about & reach out—
this, their collaborative outreach to us,
    the people,
pulling no punches that politics of the day has failed
                        We the People.
What has happened to America?
he said was the question they were asked over & over
from almost the moment they arrived in Europe,
    on a trip.

                    What a statement
both had made, what a powerful statement—
Apparently the San Francisco press, when the exhibit
was shown in The City two years earlier,
was too afraid to even make mention
    of it.

                    And if you looked down
at your feet, could you have missed
the stickers that said "Fragile" literally plastered across
    every square foot of the floor?

Sheila's Outrage – Outreach
paintings & sculpture by
Sheila Halligan-Waltz / Eike Waltz
The Mill Gallery
131 B Front St., Santa Cruz
October 2006

The Day Gilda Died

                    Yesterday, Friday, January 4,
the biggest winter storm in two years
swept through the entire region,
winds of 60 mph recorded in Santa Cruz,
over a 100 mph in the Bay Area;
driving rains fell for hours beginning the night before
—almost 10 inches drenched the Santa Cruz Mountains—;
heavy surf slammed the beaches, no color had the ocean but gray
& the churning white water of pounding wave…

                                Trees went down,
houses & cars—many reports of—crushed by trees;
power poles & lines went down, transformers blown, outages peaking
for over two million—our power went out in the morning
& would not be restored for days, we were told—
Accidents, of course, roads & highways closed, Highway 17
was closed north & south during parts of the day…

                      And Gilda Stagnaro,
yesterday morning about 9 am, at age 83,
was walking up to the restaurant on the Santa Cruz Municipal Wharf,
the one bearing her name, Gilda's, as she had done for years,
& in the wind & rain, in the storm that engulfed us all,
    as the surf swelled to thunder all around
—she loved days like this on the wharf, she always said—,
'bout 90 feet away, she collapsed & died.

                      'Queen of the wharf' she was,
for more than 35 years, working up to 16-18 hours a day,
running the well-known family restaurant there,
willing to serve, whatever it took, in all capacities she worked,
    her passsion was a life lived on the wharf—
Warm to everyone, as it was said of her, welcoming all,
all the regulars of the restaurant considered as family,
she was a tradition of her own.

>   She had always said too,
> *she wanted to die with her boots on*
>   *at the wharf,*
> said nephew Geoffrey Dunn
>   (an apt Aries attitude).

>   The storm
> forced closure of the wharf about noon,
> an extremely rare event indeed, she would not have wished
>   to have seen.
> This very day, though, this very morning,
>   there, at the wharf,
>   she had already passed on.

Gilda Stagnaro 3/31/1924 – 1/4/2008
January 5, 2008

Jack O'Neill Memorial Paddle Out

On Sunday morning, July 9,
an hour before the ceremony was to begin,
    they started to gather—
They gathered by the thousands, in the largest traditional
paddle out memorial Santa Cruz had ever seen.

                Thousands gathered
that gray & gray foggy morning, to honor surfing legend,
wetsuit pioneer, & entrepreneur, Jack O'Neill—
They gathered at Pleasure Point, on the cliffs of East Cliff Drive,
amassing all along where Jack lived at the end of 36th Avenue,
his perch on Monterey Bay, above Capitola, close by The Hook.
The ocean a monotone gray, a slight cresting swell was all
the surf there was; both air & water at 57°…

    Jack O'Neill died June 2, at 94.
He was a household name in Santa Cruz,
his eye-patch pirate countenance an immediately recognized icon;
he was famous, a symbol, in every surfing community worldwide.
His love of the sport started at Ocean Beach, in San Francisco,
in the cold Pacific waters…cold enough that he was inspired
to find a solution to staying longer in the water…
                After many experiments & prototypes,
he invented the neoprene wetsuit & set up his first shop,
    there, in San Francisco.
Then, in 1959, he moved down to Santa Cruz & opened
his second shop, simply called "Surf Shop," at Cowell Beach,
which became the local surfers' meeting place,
and he continued to develop & improve his wetsuit design,
his marketing slogan would come to claim,
    It is always summer on the inside.
A thriving surfing industry he started over the years grew;
within 20 years he was a Santa Cruz legend,
transforming The Cruz into a Surf City culture.

He was a surfer, a sailor, a business magnate,
a hot air balloonist, among other accomplishments,
and how he so much loved the ocean, a beautiful living reality
    was the ocean to him;
and how he loved to introduce others
to the mystery & magnificence of the ocean—
His *O'Neill Sea Odyssey* catamaran hosted
up to that time some 94,000 students
from all around the region
to come & experience the incredibly rich life
of our beloved Pacific Ocean.

                  Down they streamed—
Down stairs at First Peak, 36th & 38th Avenues,
surfers by the dozens & dozens carried their boards,
such various colors standing out against the gray—
At the bottom of the stairs by the dozens they launched
into the soft roll of sea, streaming out by the dozens
& dozens, out into the kelp bed…growing to hundreds,
& more hundreds, a stream of small dark figures slowly
making their way across the gray into the fog void…
wetsuit-clad surfers & paddle boarders & bogie boarders,
      streaming & streaming out—
                  They say over two thousand
were out in the water that morning,
& they brought with them thousands of flowers…
An armada of boats joined them too, some 80 or so—
sailboats, cabin cruisers, canoes, & coastal patrol,
all would surround O'Neill's double-mast wooden schooner,
the *Marie Celine*, with family members aboard,
& nearby too the 65-ft. catamaran *Sea Odyssey*—
An enormous circle of figures & boats they all formed
out upon the gray slate sea.
                          And thousands, of all ages,
gathered there, along that whole stretch of East Cliff;
they lined the railing running along the top of the cliff,
to watch & be part of this historic day.

     And just as
the ceremony began, 11 am,
the first Sun broke through, blue of sky appeared,
  conch shells were blown,
& Shaun Tomson, 1977 world surfing champion,
broadcast a memorial eulogy to all there,
with surfers sitting on their boards in that enormous circle,
arms outstretched, hands reaching, touching,
a continuous encircling chain of tribute & honor—
And then the ritual splashing & splashing of water
with hands, and untold flower petals, orchids & leis,
were thrown out upon the surf.
        Later,
a dedication ceremony renamed
the small, so-called Dirt Farm parcel
that Jack owned next to his house,
  Jack O'Neill Park.

     And surfers honored him
in paddle-out memorials around the world…

Jack O'Neill 3/27/1923 – 6/2/2017
(July) / December 2017

I Look at a Map

I look at a map of the entire world on the wall
& huge continents I see, & the vast, other world realms
    of the blue of the oceans—
So many countries I see, so many teeming-with-humanity,
    & great cultured cities among cities;
so much history, so much renown, so many famous places,
    so many well-known names,
& so why, *why*, you might ask, should the Mythos of this time
    have been born here
                     in Santa Cruz?

    The Mythos begins somewhere
    & must begin with someone

Places are timed for Vision that births the Mythos—
What it requires is that individual
    uniquely prepared
                 for that timing
        to receive it.
There is about a place
—its geography, qualities, history, people,
    its ruling God or Goddess—
that is womb for the birth of the Mythos needed
    for its time,
and Santa Cruz *is* such a place
               for this time.
And there will always be an individual…
    or two…or three…

              I have provided
weavings of the tapestry of place,
    a context,
        a soil,
that the birth of The Mythos
defining the unfolding of the New Age
we might live to see—

             And this Mythos
         precisely required
     that the soil from which it grew
         be woven
             of all the Threads
                 coming through.

I am now going out to all the world
    to speak this Mythos,
to share the Vision of Psyche
that so many years ago was given to me...
given to me upon the destined cliffs
                of The Cruz,
& I believe others, over time,
will eventually come to join me—
Will we not then boldly say,
all of us, together,
    We are going out to all the world,
    sharing our Vision,
    its Mythos coming through,
    with all the world.

September 2004

The Soul of The Cruz

Keep Santa Cruz Weird—
We heard the slogan years ago.
And Santa Cruz was a place
of all things weird, alright.
An old freedom-haven hippie town,
a highly individual soul inside this town,
full of independent souls, furiously creative,
bizarrely creative, quirky & innovative,
    in a thousand ways—
Whatever is whatever always goes in this town.
Hundreds of artists, writers, poets, musicians
compose the soul of The Cruz…& of course,
    the ocean-loving surfers too.
They all keep the soul of The Cruz alive.

        On The Edge of civilization,
yes, it is a place of decadent Postmodern,
but a place always holding the promise
    of Vision—
The Ocean of Vision, after all, is just beyond.
Over the years, a laidback fairyland to get lost in,
to break down in, to find self & be reborn.
And The Cruz is a Libra town, an Aphrodite town—
Goddess of beauty & the arts rules here.
But—but—the soul of The Cruz is surrounded
in an establishment-minded, money dictating
    milieu,
how the new wealth came in after the Quake
& changed the persona we all once knew,
buying up property, it quickly came to be
so expensive to live here, the homeless
    set up camp everywhere.
And yet the soul of The Cruz still survives,
    still survives…
& the dream of a new Mythos of the Age
    still thrives.

So what is Santa Cruz now? Some say
a bedroom community to Silicon Valley.
I say, look deeper—its soul is still here.

October 2021

About the Author

 Ron Lampi is a visionary New Age philosopher-poet, writer, and astrologer. Over the years, he has lectured on various subjects, and has been a facilitator of discussion groups. His published works thus far are only the beginning of the many manuscripts he has yet to publish. The massive project *The Mythos* is already composed of a number of books. He has lived in Santa Cruz, California, at The Edge, for over 40 years.

www.ingramcontent.com/pod-product-compliance
Lightning Source LLC
Chambersburg PA
CBHW031612160426
43196CB00006B/106